T0354874

Democracy
Held Hostage:

How neocon arrogance, George Bush's incompetence and Dick Cheney's criminality subverted the Constitution, destroyed Iraq and weakened America.

Letters to the Editor 2004-2008

by George Duncan

Order this book online at www.trafford.com
or email orders@trafford.com

Most Trafford titles are also available at major online book retailers.

Note for Librarians: A cataloguing record for this book is available from Library
and Archives Canada at www.collectionscanada.ca/amicus/index-e.html

Printed in Victoria, BC, Canada.

ISBN: 978-1-4269-1343-3 (sc)

*Our mission is to efficiently provide the world's finest, most comprehensive
book publishing service, enabling every author to experience success.
To find out how to publish your book, your way, and have it available
worldwide, visit us online at www.trafford.com*

Trafford rev. 9/2/2009

www.trafford.com

North America & international
toll-free: 1 888 232 4444 (USA & Canada)
phone: 250 383 6864 ♦ fax: 812 355 4082

"When my country…was set on fire about my ears, it was time to stir. It was time for every man to stir."

-- Thomas Paine

Foreword

My first letters came in the runup to the 2004 elections. I had been watching the conservative leadership in Congress systematically slash many of the services and benefits that had been built up during the Clinton administration. Veteran's benefits, Head Start, the privatization of Medicare, plus Bush's plan to privatize Social Security, the devastating Bush tax cut designed to bleed the government of any ability to help people and more. Frankly, I was frightened by this assault on my government which, despite Reagan and Bush Sr., is still basically a liberal democratic institution. I also was disbelieving of the need to invade Iraq. The various warnings that came along with the intelligence was apparent to me – and many others – even then.

I felt I needed to do something to at least draw attention to these abuses, especially since the mainstream media seemed oblivious to most of it. In New Hampshire especially, our entire Congressional delegation was Republican and since most of the abuses we're seeing almost daily now are a direct result of one-party rule, I thought that if people saw more clearly what these conservatives are really about, we might be able to elect Democrats. Initially, of course, I was convinced we could defeat Bush for the presidency in 2004.

Since my work and other matters keep me pretty much tied to the computer, I am unable to make commitments to activism as conducted by local and national progressive organizations beyond an occasional contribution. But since I am a copywriter, I can write letters. Since then, one letter has led to the next one, just as each Bush administration excess has led to the next one.

On occasion, someone will accuse me of "Bush bashing." It is conservatism that I see as a dangerous disease infecting the nation. Not Republicanism, mind you, but conservatism, which is not the same thing. Most of my letters, as you will see, are not personal diatribes, but arrows pointing to commentary from such authoritative sources as *The New York Times*, *The Washington Post*, and *The Los Angeles Times*, Web sites like Truthout.org, Salon.com and Slate.com, a few progressive blogs and so on. In each case, these commentaries are presented inside quote marks and with attribution, plus an observation or two on the matter by me.

Far more the case, however, is that hardly a day has passed since I began writing these weekly letters that someone hasn't complimented them and told me to "keep it up." That's the most satisfying result. Another is that since my letters started appearing in our two local weeklies, the letters section in those papers have grown markedly with other writers expressing their views on the current political or military debacles. If my letters have encouraged them to speak out, I am most gratified.

A number of motives have been imputed to George W. Bush for starting the Iraq war, from neocon hubris to the Bush family oil interests. I believe no small factor in that decision matrix was Bush's awareness that Americans tend not to switch presidents during a war so he made himself a "war president" to help assure his reelection – which, clearly it did.

Whatever the reason, the Iraq war – and especially the incompetence with which it has been prosecuted – added to Bush's irresponsible tax cuts, his blatant attack on social security, his arrogant attempt to break down the constitutional separation of church and state, his illegal institution of a militaristic, secret government and more make me want to cry out for justice, for honesty and some semblance of common sense.

George Duncan

Acknowledgements

I owe a great debt to the many writers, editors and commentators I have encountered on the Internet on progressive web sites and blogs whose observations have inspired me, especially those I have quoted in my letters.

I also wish to thank the many people of Peterborough, NH who have encouraged me to continue writing, and the editors of the *Monadnock Ledger and Transcript, The Keene Sentinel* and others who have graciously published the letters. Thanks go too, to my late wife Sally for putting up with my frequent preoccupation and for her thoughtful assistance.   GD.

2004

COMMON SENSE;

ADDRESSED TO THE

INHABITANTS

OF

AMERICA,

On the following interesting

SUBJECTS.

I. Of the Origin and Design of Government in general, with concise Remarks on the English Constitution.

II. Of Monarchy and Hereditary Succession.

III. Thoughts on the present State of American Affairs.

IV. Of the present Ability of America, with some miscellaneous Reflections.

Man knows no Master save creating HEAVEN,
Or those whom choice and common good ordain.

THOMSON.

PHILADELPHIA;

Printed, and Sold, by R. BELL, in Third-Street.

MDCCLXXVI.

This or That?

The chief executive of an American corporation is required by law to "sign off" on the financial statements made in his company's annual report. He must <u>certify</u> that the numbers are accurate. Not just what the accountants told him, or what the CFO said, but he, as the senior responsible officer of the company, <u>certifies</u> that they are correct.

Is it expecting too much, therefore, for the President of The United States to verify the information his intelligence people are giving him -- knowing as he should, the often ambiguous nature of intelligence -- before invading a foreign country, expending great amounts of American treasure, killing many thousands of innocent Iraqis and sending our young men and women into circumstances where some (now almost 1000) are sure to be killed and many more to return with grievous, life-altering wounds?

There are only two possibilities. Either President Bush deliberately and knowingly manipulated the intelligence information he received in order to justify his invasion of Iraq – in which case he is guilty of war crimes; or he was, as he claims, misled by his intelligence people and failed to verify the information – despite the numerous caveats it contained. In that case, he is at the very least an irresponsible chief executive even by ordinary business standards, and in my view, unfit to be president.

As the song says, "It's gotta be this or that."

George Duncan
Peterborough, NH

8.7.04

War-Time Presidents?

I've never understood where the idea came from that Democrats are less militarily committed to the protection of our country than Republicans. On the Republican side, there was the intrepid 90-day Invasion of Grenada under Ronald Reagan – as Oliver North's Contra death squads gallantly opposed the democratically elected government of Nicaragua. There was Bush senior's two-week invasion of Panama to kidnap Noriega, and his 45-day defense of Kuwait in Desert Storm. And now we have Bush junior's highly questionable adventure in Iraq.

Contrast that record, dubious at best, with the prosecution of World War I, by Woodrow Wilson, a Democrat. And World War II, which was prosecuted by Franklin D. Roosevelt, *the* Democrat. The Korean Conflict was prosecuted by Harry Truman, also a Democrat (also the only person to ever drop an A-bomb, ending WWII). Democrat John F. Kennedy carried out Eisenhower's flawed invasion of Cuba, and sent military advisors to Vietnam. The Vietnam War, outcome aside, was prosecuted by Lyndon Johnson, another Democrat. (It was left to the Republican Nixon to secretly bomb Cambodia and then lie about it.) Even the anti-hero Clinton sent troops to Haiti and Somalia and tried to take out bin Laden. Am I missing something?

George Duncan
Peterborough, NH

8.16.04

Fool me once, but <u>five</u> times?

It wouldn't be too surprising if a politically ambitious soldier were to exaggerate the nature of a combat injury with an eye on a future campaign. There have been examples of politicians and others claiming awards they never received. Nor would it be impossible for the U.S. Navy to wink and blink if given a heads-up by some politically powerful insider regarding the awarding of a particular medal. But FIVE TIMES? Come on. Even the U.S. Navy isn't that stupid. Or irresponsible. Nor is the Department of Defense, Rumsfeld notwithstanding. Besides, John Kerry's war record isn't some unsupported claim. The official citations are available on the Internet (Johnkerry.com) to anyone who wants to read them. All five of them. Signed by the appropriate U.S. Navy and Pentagon authorities. Three Purple Hearts, (One Purple Heart and two gold stars in lieu of the 2nd and 3rd Purple Hearts to be exact), a Bronze Star, and a Silver Star? All five fabricated?

As they say in Texas, "That dawg won't hunt." What's going on here is a degree of hatred seldom seen in a national spotlight. Men who feel betrayed by a former comrade who, repulsed by what he saw, spoke out against the barbarities of the Vietnam War. John Kerry violated the code of silence around that war and these men, paid and encouraged by conservative activist Robert Perry, thought they'd found a way to pay him back. Just another chapter in the Republican Book of Dirty Tricks. How pathetic.

George Duncan
Peterborough, NH

8.18.04

Yes, you *can* fool all of the people, all of the time.

You can fool all of the people all of the time – if no one knows what you're doing. Unfortunately, that's the direction our flow of information has taken in the last year or more, with cable networks caving in to administration contentions on a wide range of issues from the environment to jobs to healthcare to Iraq. Some individual journalists may be liberal, but more and more, they work for conservative media conglomerates. Recently, both *The Washington Post* and the *NY Times* acknowledged that they had been negligent in their coverage of administration claims leading up to the war. This is less true of Internet media. One outstanding source of articles drawn from the U.S. and foreign press is Truthout.org. You can sign up there for an email service that will bring you 6-8 items of interest each weekday. President Bush's brag that he doesn't read newspapers is all the more reason the rest of us need to.

George Duncan
Peterborough, NH

8.18.04

What, exactly, did Bush do?

I wish someone could tell me exactly what it is President Bush did in relation to September 11th that was so fantastic. Rudy Giuliani (sage of all things 9/11) says he remained "rock solid." What does that mean? I thought the 7-minute stare with "My Pet Goat" looked more frozen than rock solid. Does it mean Bush didn't then fall down in a heap on the floor, weeping? I recall his visiting the site in N.Y. and jumping into a fab photo opp with a firefighter, yelling into a megaphone, "they'll hear from us!" or immortal words to that effect. I remember his Churchillian challenge, "bring it on." Then he spent a good deal of time and effort trying to blame the attack on Iraq, all evidence to the contrary. What else? Oh yes. Osama somebody.

George Duncan
Peterborough, NH

8.31.04

Convention

Well, what is there to say about an orgy of hate? Perhaps a few points are worth noting for those who haven't connected the dots. There was Arnold Schwarzenegger, the self-made cartoon, telling us that anyone who is concerned about the economy is a "girlyman." He also pathetically tried to puff up his resume by lying about leaving Austria as a child under the guns of Russian tanks – which subsequent research has demonstrated didn't exist, his having been born two years after the Soviets left. I thought his jutting jaw and flag-waving cliches were a good take on Joseph Goebbels, though. The Man from Halliburton was his predictable, smarmy self, spewing out the same old lies and distortions as though by repeating them often enough, he'll make them true. George Bush was, as usual, all hat and no cattle.

But the star of the show was clearly ZigZag Zell. I haven't seen such demagoguery since Broderick Crawford won the Oscar for "All the King's Men." He actually said that our nation was being torn apart because of "a Democrat's manic obsession to bring down our commander in chief." It's called an election, Zell. Get over it. But these issues are beside the point. Connecting the dots means identifying the meaning these events hold when the balloons have all come down and the crowd has moved on. I could never synthesize that meaning half so well as Paul Krugman did in his 9/3 *New York Times* column: "Nothing makes you hate people as much as knowing in your heart that you are in the wrong and they are in the right. But the vitriol also reflects the fact that many of the people at that convention, for all their flag-waving, hate America. They want a controlled, monolithic society; they fear and loathe our nation's freedom, diversity and complexity." I can only pray that, come November, my Republican friends will recall Mr. Miller's hate-filled face, the swift boat assassins' lies, the arrogance and duplicity with which the Iraq war was begun and prosecuted, and say to themselves, "I'm better than that."

George Duncan
Peterborough, NH

9.9.04

Foreign Countries

It may be instructive to take a look at how people in the rest of the world are responding to the American presidential campaign. In a nutshell, large majorities in 30 of 35 countries surveyed prefer John Kerry. A global survey was conducted by GlobeScan, Inc., a global research firm, and the University of Maryland. 34,330 people were surveyed. The only countries favoring Bush were the Philippines, Nigeria and Poland. The majorities are striking. Norway, 74% Kerry to Bush's 7%. Germany; 74% to 10%; France, 64% to 5 %; The Netherlands, 63% to 6%; Italy, 58% to 14%; Spain 45% to 7%. Even our erstwhile partner in Iraq, Great Britain, favors Kerry 47% to 16% as did most of the other countries who have contributed troops to Iraq. All nine countries polled in Latin America prefer Kerry by similar margins.

Why is that? Because, I think, these people have not been seduced by American media. They are able to assess the candidates more objectively, unburdened by Wolf Blitzer's blithe acceptance of non-answers to his non-questions. They are not affected by the relentless beat of the swift Bush liars and the ugly excesses of talk radio. Individually, they carry no partisan baggage and are untainted by partisan rhetoric.

Ultimately, of course, in countries where the stones once echoed to the dictator's rant and the policeman's knock, they recognize the innate hostility of America's imperialist foreign policy, as driven by the neocon cabal that's advising Bush – or perhaps we should say, running him.

George Duncan
Peterborough, NH

9.12.04

Dumbest Election

A leading web publisher (Truthout.org) recently described the current election campaign as the "Dumbest. Election. Ever." Clearly, the quality of public debate on critical issues has deteriorated, thanks largely to television, where talking heads have become shouting heads, and what used to be discussion shows have evolved into what can only be described as "politainment."

On TV today, the main topic of discussion is the invective being hurled by the campaigns' latest ads. If an issue can't be expressed in a sound bite, it's simply ignored. How else explain Bush's continued success in the polls as the "war president" while the war he started descends deeper every day into an utter chaos of death and destruction. Apparently so far as the TV generation is concerned, Bush's flight suit trumps Kerry's wind surfing, even if Iraq explodes into civil war. But to quote the Truthout.org publisher again, "look into the eyes of those 1,000 lost faces and tell me they don't deserve better than this stupid election and its stupid public debate."

We can give them better by looking past the sound bites, the ads and the lies, past Bush's ludicrous "catastrophic success" at the only thing that matters -- what's really happening on the ground.

George Duncan
Peterborough, NH

9.22.04

Drunk Driving

As a talk show caller put it recently, "Just because you give someone the keys to your car, doesn't mean you're giving them permission to drive it drunk." John Kerry voted to give Bush the means to fight the war in Iraq, but not to drive it into a ditch – and lose more than 1000 American lives in the process. Kerry didn't expect Bush to go to war with a reduced force to satisfy Rumsfeld's pet theories, then to bypass Fallujah and other key cities in the Sunni Triangle in a mad dash for Baghdad solely for its public relations effect. He didn't give Bush permission to go to war without an exit strategy. He didn't vote to go to war with virtually no international support (sorry, Togo). And Kerry never voted to trash what was left of our nation's image in the world by negating every international treaty in sight, insulting our allies and condoning the torture of prisoners. Then Bush declares "mission accomplished" and blithely ignores accountability for everything that's happened since (except, of course, for his ludicrous claim of "catastrophic success"). This is a war president?

George Duncan
Peterborough, NH

9.27.04

Where is the line?

The New York Times, ever the good grey lady, describes Bush's smear tactics as "un-American." OK, that's true enough – but it doesn't begin to make the point. What kind of president, candidate -- or man -- insults the intelligence of the American people with lies about the facts surrounding his policies and decision-making – and then persists in those lies despite mounting evidence to the contrary? This past Sunday's story (NYT 10/3) about the aluminum tubes that were presented as being for nuclear centrifuges despite U.S. scientists' repeated cautions is just a recent example. What kind of arrogance does it take to shrug off a "partial election" and present it as democratic because the security situation your actions created simply won't support a free and open election? Think the Sunnis won't mind being left out? Think that makes the results legitimate? Come on, Mr. Bush, we can read!

What this administration has shown for all of us since day one is contempt. Contempt for the rule of law, contempt for the truth, contempt for our right to know the truth and for our ability to discern the truth without Bush's spin. (Like Kofi Annan's 9/16 interview on BBC in which he declared the Iraq invasion <u>illegal</u> by UN Charter standards– while Bush goes on pretending it was to protect UN interests!)

Last week's debate showed that Bush thinks that if he just says something often enough and forcefully enough, it becomes truth—because he said it. When does this guy go over the line? Is there still a line left in American politics? Do conservatives want to win so desperately that they will abandon basic principles of common honesty and decency? John Kerry may not be Michael the Archangel, but last week he showed himself to be a man of principle, of vision and courage. A man we can trust to bring us out of this quagmire with honor and take our country forward.

George Duncan
Peterborough

10.03.04

Remember the Neocons

Those who plan to vote for Bush in November need to remember they'll also be voting for Richard Perle, Paul Wolfowitz, Douglas Feith, Lewis Libby and others in the neocon cabal that has taken over the defense department. Rumsfeld is their figurehead and Cheney the puppet master who keeps telling Bush Iraq is just a faith-based initiative. This is a dangerous crowd, and their promise is for more of the same, leading our country down the road to what they hope will be a democratic hegemony in the Middle East. (And you see how great their judgement has been so far.)

The beginnings of their totalitarianism is visible now in the Patriot Act and the various rules or lack of rules governing the detention or arrest of whomever the government decides is "suspicious." You can see it in the National Intelligence Database that gives investigators unprecedented access to a wide range of personal information on American citizens – no court order required. You can see it in the prisoner abuse at Abu Ghraib. Some say Ashcroft is just waiting for another attack to unveil Patriot II. All he needs now is a brown shirt and an armband. Do you really want to give these people license to pursue their imperialist agenda? Think twice. You can only vote once.

George Duncan
Peterborough, NH

10.03.04

Theater of the Absurd?

So the president "recovered" from his earlier debacle. Wow! I guess that means we have to give him another shot at destroying the country. Ours, not Iraq, though likely that too. Yes sir, in place of the clueless stare, we got 90 minutes of swaggering winks. Instead of stuttering repetitions, we got the genuine Bush sarcasm with a dash of aggressive staging. That said, should we really be electing the Leader of the Free World based on our perceptions of a few 90-minute platform performances and the media spin that accompanies them? Or should we look beyond the theatrics at the records of the candidates, and the promise their policies represent? Bush is obvious. The record? One failed initiative after another in Iraq. The promise? More of the same. What mistakes?

How anyone can look to this man as a guardian of the nation's security is beyond me. Kerry's record? Courageous personal defense of America, both in and out of uniform, followed by twenty years of thoughtful negotiation and policy shaping in the Senate. The promise? Most likely more of the same. Thoughtful negotiations with our allies around the world – once the poisonous Bush is out of the way – to show them where their true interests lie and bring them back to the table. The future war against the terrorists, as Kerry began to point out, but didn't have time to finish, will be one, not of shock and awe bombing raids, but of hard nosed intelligence work which will, in turn, require highly cooperative relationships with all the nations where Al Qaeda plants its roots. All the nations that, if Bush is reelected, won't give him the time of day. Without that, we'll be sitting ducks. It's up to us.

George Duncan
Peterborough, NH

10.11.04

16

Why there's no flu vaccine

Despite numerous warnings over the last few years, the Bush administration did nothing about the impending shortage of flu vaccine because conservative ideology prefers to leave such matters to the "marketplace" or to private corporations to profit therefrom. But there isn't much profit in flu vaccine, so the "marketplace" took a pass. It was Calvin Coolidge who famously said, "The business of America is business," and the Republican party that has taken it for its mantra, placing the interests of business ahead of the interests of people at every opportunity. Privatize the military so business can profit from war at taxpayers expense. Introduce private investment accounts into Social Security so business can profit at the expense of retirees. Turn Medicare over to the pharmaceutical companies so they can treat their bottom lines with our tax money. Keep prescription drugs from crossing the Canadian border under the guise of "safety" so they can't compete with US pharmas. Limit healthcare insurance to catastrophic coverage and let people fend for themselves with so-called "Medical Savings Accounts" meaning you pay for the rest of it. Introduce "flex-time" in the workplace to relieve employers of the need to pay overtime and further impoverish working families. Destroy the public school system in order to take down the teacher's union. Promote outsourcing to help corporations lower costs by sending the few good manufacturing jobs left overseas to be replaced by service jobs that pay significantly less, have no healthcare or other benefits. I'm as pro-business as the next guy. I make my living from business just as you do. In fact, my business is helping other businesses. But people have to come first, or what's business for? John Kerry and the Democrats put people first.

George Duncan
Peterborough, NH

10.25.04

Let's Learn to Think for Ourselves

There was a report last week that the Bush campaign in West Virginia sent letters to Christian fundamentalist groups telling them that if the Democrats won the election, they would ban the bible. Putting aside what that says about the Republicans' respect for the intelligence of their fundamentalist "base," until we all learn to examine issues and ask questions for ourselves, distortions and lies of that sort -- and there were many more examples throughout the campaign – can only deepen the cultural and social attitudes which the post-election pundits say divide us. If they are right, it's disappointing that an issue like gay marriage could trump such critical realities as the debacle in Iraq, the deepening deficit, the jobless economy, problems in healthcare and education and more, but that appears to be the case. So what to do about it? We have to talk to each other. If you think Democrats would ban the bible, ask them about it. If you believe someone else's gay marriage will somehow affect yours, talk with a gay couple. You may discover they're more like you than you thought.

George Duncan
Peterborough, NH

11.05.04

Cult of Personality?

President Bush says he'll reach out to those in Congress *who agree with him*.

It's obvious from his recent appointments that the secrecy and conformist environment that marked his first administration will only intensify in his second. The president is clearly surrounding himself with faithful retainers. People who are likely to value their close, personal relationships with Bush above any contrary opinions they may harbor in the development of the policies that will shape this country's future in the years ahead. Every president wants partisans in his cabinet. And normally, that's not a problem. But in this case, judgements like invading Iraq on questionable and conflicting intelligence reports, attempting an occupation with insufficient force, initially bypassing Falluja in order to achieve a pr victory in Baghdad (John McCain said on Sunday that Falluja was "a base of operations we never should have allowed to build up in the first place."), misjudging the response of the Iraqis to our presence there, supporting the wrong people to help form a democratic government. All these failures and others could have been averted if the president had been freely advised by responsible people. People responsible to you and me, and to the oath of office they took, not to Bush/Cheney and their radical ideology. Even Porter Goss at the CIA has ordered his people to "support" the administration, not advise it. We are perilously close to a cult of personality (or at least of ideology) in the White House, which is dangerous enough, but to make it worse, the Bush cult bathes itself in the self-justifications of theocratic rectitude.

George Duncan
Peterborough, NH

11.22.04

Cult of Arrogance

Princeton economist Paul Krugman warns that Bush's economic policies are turning the U.S. into the fiscal equivalent of a banana republic. The current plunge in the U.S. dollar, augmented by Bush's pigheaded insistence on more tax cuts and "privatizing" social security, despite the warnings of many economic experts right and left, is just another example of the arrogance that has marked this administration from the beginning. It was a similar "privatizing" plan in the 90s that helped to drive Argentina to a $100 billion default in 2001. "This is a group of people who don't believe that any of the rules really apply," Krugman told Reuters. "They are utterly irresponsible." In the months ahead, you and I need to watch Senators Gregg and Sununu and Congressman Bass to see how they respond – or don't – to these and other outrages taking place. Do they have any sense of responsibility beyond party and ideology? (How did Bass vote in the recent DeLay debacle? Would he be willing to do the right thing and insist DeLay step aside if he's indicted, despite the rules change? Could our local newspaper provide some independent coverage of our representatives and what they're doing in Congress?)

George Duncan
Peterborough, NH

11.28.04

Moral Values

Now that the emotions of the moment have passed, and the election tea leaves are becoming clearer, it seems that the crimson tide some thought might be about to swallow us all like Jonah in the whale may turn out to be less than biblical. England's Economist magazine -- clearly neither a red state nor a blue state publication – ran a study of their own which found that while 22% of those surveyed did indeed give "moral values" as a factor in their vote, that number was actually down from the 35% who said so in 2000 and the 40% who claimed moral values in 1996. So apparently, "Desperate Housewives" is safe – and remains a top rated hit throughout America's moral heartland.

Further, in a recent AP poll, 60% of Americans (cutting across all class and income levels) want to see Roe V. Wade kept exactly as it is, while just 30% would like it overturned. Even among Republicans, evangelists and people over 65 less than 50% opposed Roe. So the simpler and more reasonable key to the election may be that President Bush was, as he reminded us every ten seconds, a "war president," and history has shown that voters are reluctant to switch ponies in mid-conflict. Of course, one way to assure that you'll be a war president come election time is to start your own war. That may or may not have occurred to Mr. Bush but you can bet it sure isn't beneath Mr. Rove. As that other political operative, Hermann Goering, once said, "It is the leaders of the country that determine the policy, and it is always a simple matter to drag the people along, whether it is a democracy, or a fascist dictatorship, or a parliament or a communist dictatorship. Voice or no voice, the people can always be brought to the bidding of the leaders. All you have to do is to tell them they are being attacked." Orange alert!

George Duncan
Peterborough, NH

12.05.04

Humvees

Know why Rumsfeld never fixed the humvees? Because to do something about them would have been admitting the basic mistake that was made from day one: the response of the Iraqis to our invasion that was promised by the neocon morons who dreamed up this whole debacle. They said we'd be welcomed with flowers. So the humvees that raced to Baghdad were basically transportation vehicles. Light and fast as humvees are supposed to be. Suddenly, when the flowers turned into bombs, the humvees became combat vehicles. For Rummy to then replace the humvees with tanks and/or add more troops or do anything else that made sense, would be to admit the Big Mistake. Whoops! No WMD over there. No Al Qaeda over here. Nothing but thousands of P.O.'d Iraqis who want us out of their country – and armed to the teeth with the tons of unprotected ordinance they stole right from under our noses. Indeed, that inability to admit to any mistake, that lack of accountability, is the hallmark of this administration. Instead of truth we get imagery. John Wayne yelling threats through a bullhorn at Ground Zero. Tom Cruise landing on the deck of a carrier under a "Mission Accomplished" banner. How about a war president visiting the wounded? Well, no. Attending a military funeral? Uh-uh. Might remind people our soldiers are dying and being maimed so the neocons can shove democracy down the throats of a theocratic society that doesn't want it. Looks like Bush and Company are suffering from the same problem that inflicts those who elected him; too much television.

George Duncan
Peterborough, NH

12.12.04

Social Security

The Republicans have been gunning for Social Security since the day it passed the Congress in 1935. They just can't stand the idea of their taxes being used to help others survive. Clearly, some adjustments need to be made. So Bush intends to take this opportunity to throw the baby out with the bath water and "privatize" Social Security, the first step in turning the whole program over to the bankers and brokers – and getting it out from under the "full faith and credit of the U.S. government." Never mind that it will cost taxpayers trillions more in debt. Never mind that those investments won't be guaranteed in any way. Never mind that many recipients never get to complete their own programs for various legitimate reasons and will be left short. And just wait till the investment con artists get their hands on this one! The study committee that set up the program for President Roosevelt stated, "A program of economic security, as we vision it, must have as its primary aim the assurance of an adequate income to each human being in childhood, youth, middle age, or old age -- in sickness or health. It must provide safeguards against all of the hazards leading to destitution and dependency." Note words like "assurance" and "safeguards." Try finding those in the market. In the Federalist Papers, Alexander Hamilton warned that, "a dangerous ambition more often lurks behind the specious mask of zeal for the rights of people than under the forbidding appearance of zeal for the firmness and efficiency of government." In his wonderful book, "Bowling Alone," Robert Putnam documents the erosion of community in America. Privatizing Social Security is one more giant step in that direction.

George Duncan
Peterborough, NH

12.19.04

24

Marley Was A Liberal

Early in the fateful evening of Christmas Eve, Ebenezer Scrooge is visited by two local businessmen seeking contributions for the poor. Upon learning Scrooge's partner, Jacob Marley, is deceased, they state hopefully, "We have no doubt his *liberality* is well represented by his surviving partner." At the ominous word "liberality", Scrooge frowns, shakes his head, and hands back the man's credentials. "Are there no prisons?" Scrooge asks. "Can't the churches and soup kitchens take care of them?" Bush asked.

Later, when Marley's ghost appears in his room, Scrooge reminds him, "But you were always a good man of business, Jacob." "Business!" cries Marley. "Mankind was my business; charity, mercy, forbearance and benevolence were, all, my business. The dealings of my trade were but a drop of water in the comprehensive ocean of my business!" he exclaims, and then berates himself for not having done more for his fellow beings while he lived. Those are Democratic moral values. "Bleeding heart" liberal values. Why? Because liberals believe that just as a chain is only as strong as its weakest link, so a society is only as strong and vibrant as its weakest members. So we seek to overcome the Scrooge-like tendencies we all share ("It's your money, keep it!") by bringing the power and capacities of government to the task of helping those weakest among us to survive, to grow and ultimately, to contribute. Idealistic? Perhaps. But realistic, too. Imperfect? You bet. But still just a drop of water in the ocean of this nation's business.

George Duncan
Peterborough, NH

12.27.04

2005

Town Meeting: Democracy in Action

Call me crazy, but it seems to me that when property taxes are increasing, and budgets are going up, that's a time for greater discussion of costs and needs, not less. It's a time for a community to come together and be sure we understand the reasons for this or that expenditure before we approve it. It's a time when Selectmen should be able to explain their decisions to whatever extent is necessary. Where town boards can offer their unique perspectives to concerned citizens. (We got some surprises on those scores last year!) That's the kind of dialog that can only happen at Town Meeting where facts can be clearly laid out for all to share. I recall, just a few months ago, the Peterborough Verbatim chorus – a prominent realtor among them – singing, "Hear the pros, hear the cons, listen to every faction. That's democracy in action." It seemed to resonate with most folks then, and I'm sure it still does.

That's not to say there may not be ways to make Town Meeting more responsive and move things along a bit quicker, but let's not throw the baby out with the bathwater. I know I have a few ideas and I'll bet others do, too. Why not send them to the Selectmen – and make a New Year's resolution now to be there this March to "listen to every faction."

George Duncan
Peterborough, NH

1.03.05

Social Insecurity

George Bush's so-called "privatization" plan is just another attempt by conservatives to shut down one of the country's most successful progressive programs. Even the prestigious Concord Coalition – hardly a liberal think tank – has said, "Ensuring a more sustainable system will require change, meaning that someone is going to have to give up something – either in the form of higher contributions, lower benefits or a combination of both. No Social Security reform will succeed unless this fact is acknowledged up front."

Giveaways to Wall Street that add trillions to the deficit would only "signal to increasingly wary financial markets that Washington has no intention of doing what is necessary to get its fiscal house in order. This would increase the risks of a so-called 'hard landing' such as a spike in interest rates, rising inflation and a plunging dollar." All of which would ensure another plunging market.

Let's get a message to Senators Gregg and Sununu and Congressman Bass. You and I are their constituents, not George Bush. And we won't think of them as any less Republican if they oppose the president's plan.

George Duncan
Peterborough, NH

1.09.05

Con Jobs

Apparently the "con" in neocon doesn't just stand for conservative. The administration has finally acknowledged what has been painfully obvious for more than a year, and which some have known from day one – there ain't no weapons of mass destruction in Iraq. Now a new BBC documentary strongly suggests that al-Qaeda may also be just another Bush bogeyman. Entitled, "The Power of Nightmares: The Rise of the Politics of Fear," Robert Scheer says in The L.A. Times that the film "makes a powerful case that Bush administration, led by a tight-knit cabal of Machiavellian neoconservatives, has seized upon the false image of a unified terrorist threat to replace the expired Soviet empire in order to push a political agenda." And Jonathan Raban writes in The NY Review of Books, "With the neocon mythmakers now in senior government positions, September 11 made it easy to cast al-Qaeda in the Evil Empire role that they had previously scripted for the Soviet Union." Like the much-vaunted Soviet threat, also lacking any hard evidence. (I often wonder if the neoconservatives ever consider how like the militant Islamists they are. Or how similar the Bush administration is to the Hussein administration, especially in working exclusively through sycophants and rejecting dissent- or even discussion?)

Now comes another Bush bogeyman – the myth of a Social Security crises and the so-called "cure" that's ultimately designed to kill the patient. Maybe this time enough sane voices are being heard to at least put the brakes on this moronic privatization idea. But maybe not. Sunday's NY Times reports Bush's order compelling Social Security Administration officials to help market the crises myth, many in violation of their own knowledge of the truth. As John F. Kennedy once said, "The great enemy of truth is very often not the lie – deliberate, contrived and dishonest – but the myth, persistent, persuasive and unrealistic."

Maybe Senators Sununu and Gregg and Congressman Bass could tell us how they see it. What do you say, gentlemen? Pro or more con?

George Duncan
Peterborough, NH

1.16.05

Don't make us come over there!…

So is it the bully pulpit or a bully president? You don't have to read between the lines to get the sub-text of Bush's new foreign policy initiative, it's right there on top: we're going to "democratize" any country we think isn't running things the way we think they ought to. Like we're democratizing Iraq. Especially those countries run by "tyrants" (our definition) and especially where the people don't look like us. This is Paul Wolfowitz & Co. speaking through Bush's mouth. The neocons are in charge. Remember these are the people who arrogantly assumed the Iraqis would welcome us with open arms. Irving Kristol, one of the neoconservative movement's founders, wrote in 2003, "…the United States will always feel obliged to defend, if possible, a democratic nation under attack from nondemocratic forces." If you don't share that sense of obligation, when your kid gets called up to defend Taiwan from nondemocratic China, or to liberate Iran, Syria, Saudi Arabia or Egypt, you can discuss it with Mr. Kristol. In her confirmation hearings, Condoleezza Rice named as "outposts of tyranny," Cuba, Burma, North Korea, Iran, Belarus and Zimbabwe. Whew! We're going to be busy!

It's been described as an "idealistic" speech. Heck, I'm a liberal and that's about as idealistic as one can get. It's supposed to be our tragic flaw. So what am I worried about? "It's not a discontinuity. It is not a right turn," says one anonymous administration official. And in his New York Times column, conservative columnist David Brooks writes, "The speech does not command us to go off on a global crusade, instantaneously pushing democracy on one and all." I dearly hope they're right. But I can't shake the concern they arouse by finding it necessary to protest so much.

George Duncan
Peterborough, NH

1.25.05

Test it!

If George Bush thinks the stock market is such a great idea for Social Security, I have a suggestion for him. In the marketing business, we don't just run out and spend huge sums of money on unproven schemes. We test them first. So why doesn't Bush have Congress change the law that prohibits the Social Security trustees from investing in stocks (wonder why they thought that was necessary?), take a portion of the trust fund and put it in the market for say, 20 years. The government's been borrowing from the fund for the last 20 years anyway. See how it works. If it does, he'll have proved his point without destroying the system. If it doesn't, there'll still be plenty of time to repay any losses since the Social Security Trustees say the system is sound until 2042. The Congressional Budget Office estimate goes ten years beyond that to 2052!

But maybe privatization is just one of those ideas whose time has gone. USA Today (7/28/2000) and the Texas Observer both report that, as a congressional candidate in 1978, George W. Bush was claiming then that "Social Security would go bust in ten years unless people were given a chance to invest the money themselves." As we know, the system has been running surpluses ever since.

Of course, on the chance Bush really cares, an easy way to fix it right now would be to raise the income cap subject to payroll tax above the present $90,000 to maybe $120,000. Voila! Tons of new money coming into the program. No risky investments, no loss of benefits. But that would inconvenience some of Bush's wealthy contributors, so it probably won't happen. It's really amazing to see how ideology trumps simple mathematics. Right Charlie?

George Duncan
Peterborough, NH

1.30.05

Preserving the Social Fabric

I was pleased that George W. Bush promised not to set an "artificial timetable" for withdrawal from Iraq. I hate those artificial things, don't you? He also said he'd keep an "open mind" on Social Security – so long as any plan includes private accounts. Like Henry Ford offering any color car – so long as it's black.

One of the strongest arguments for keeping Social Security as it is, however, has nothing to do with the numbers. It has to do with that first word, "social." Social Security endures largely because it is a shared contract among all of us. We all contribute so we all can benefit – as members of the society. Social Security binds us together in a caring culture in which we recognize our collective responsibility to one another. Even our money reminds that we are one from many (E Pluribus Unum). Yet George Bush's privatization program would destroy that social fabric – remove Social Security from joint auspices under government in a relentless march toward the "ownership society" that conservatives lust after. (I've often wondered why anyone would elect to government someone who doesn't believe in government?) The result is, instead of a seamless society, we become divided into 300 million individuals, each with his or her own walls, moat and drawbridge. That said, however, it appears that the fallacies behind Bush's attack on Social Security are becoming obvious even to his supporters, so sanity may prevail eventually.

George Duncan
Peterborough, NH

2.06.05

Keep the Drive-Through Ban

There is a line in the recent play, Peterborough Verbatim, that captures the spirit of the drive-through dilemma. It said, in effect, that people in Peterborough get to know one another at least in part because we don't have drive-throughs, allowing folks to meet one another at Nonie's, the Diner, Gatto's, Pearl, etc. The subject is coming up again as the town seeks to extend the drive-through ban to the new Village Commercial District.

When the drive-through ban was first introduced, it was accompanied by a 9-point memo that outlined many valid reasons why drive-throughs have a negative impact on the town. They included the exporting of town money to an out-of-town franchise.

And the isolation these structures impose upon all of us. How they keep people in their cars so they don't stroll through Depot Square or down Main Street or even through Peterborough Plaza, seriously reducing business traffic. Dunkin Donuts, for example, opened in a plaza where they bring business to their neighbors and don't blight our town's landscape with more macadam, exhaust, trash, etc.

Those reasons still hold, of course, but since then, we've become aware of other, pro-business reasons. Through my participation in the Economic Vitality Sub-Committee of the Master Planning Group, the Chamber's Business Support Committee and the recent Hassinger-LaPoint Business Outreach Initiative, I am aware of the generally accepted observation that businesses elect to come to Peterborough mainly because the principals involved want to live here. They come for the "Peterborough lifestyle." The minute we allow Fallen Arches and the other fast fooders to plant their drive-throughs in town (the amendment doesn't apply to banks, pharmacies or other non-restaurants), we might as well be Keeneborough, Nashuaborough or Keokukborough, for that matter. We lose a major part of our lifestyle advantage. Also, studies show that franchises are tax-negative enterprises, creating costs to the town well beyond their contribution to the tax base.

For the record, Peterborough isn't anti-business. It's anti-stupid business. Let's vote "Yes" on Zoning Amendment #3 and keep it that way. And while we're at it, let's keep Town Meeting. That's smart, too.

George Duncan
Peterborough, NH

2.20.05

Privatization? Prove it!

On TV this week, John Sununu continued to beat the privatization drum on the grounds it would preserve the Social Security program despite the fact that the president himself – among many others – has acknowledged that private accounts will not assure solvency. The conservative American Institute for Economic Research points out, "Problems abound with this (privatization) idea. Among other things, it would create pressure for the government to influence financial markets and to bail out individuals whose investments did poorly."

Other opponents include Newsweek columnist Robert Samuelson; "Judged by (the CBO's) arithmetic, Bush's Social Security program is a hoax." Laura Tyson, Dean of the London Business School (where the Brits are running from a similar system in droves); "Borrowing of this magnitude (to support the transition to private accounts) could spook global investors, triggering sharply higher interest rates on U.S. government debt and a collapsing dollar." Economists of the Brookings Institution; "(Social Security's) solvency for future generations can be ensured through modest benefit reductions and modest revenue increases." The Institute for Policy Research at Northwestern University; "The basic income to those no longer able to work can no longer be guaranteed under the Bush plan." And on and on.

But all that is really beside the point. As Joe Biden said on "Meet The Press" this week, "The issue for Bush isn't Social Security's solvency, but its legitimacy." He's trying ultimately to end it, not mend it. It's obvious to anyone who isn't a mathematical moron or an ideological hack that the elements to be adjusted are retirement age, salary cap, benefits and payroll tax.

Any legislator who supports privatization should be required to prove that it works, <u>and that the other plans don't.</u> On paper, in black and white.

George Duncan
Peterborough, NH

2.27.05

Sneak Thieves

This past week, Governor John Lynch was reported to oppose certain measures in the deceptively named "Clear Skies" Act. Well he might. Clear Skies is a Republican re-write of the Clean Air Act which guts the original act of the requirement for power plants to add new pollution controls when they expand. "The approach would allow power plants to keep operating for 100 years without applying emission controls," said Conrad Schneider of the Clean Air Task Force. How's that for "clear skies!" In addition, another provision secretly slipped into the bill would strip state attorneys general of the power to sue polluting power plants! That's the only weapon states have to combat pollution abuse!

In healthcare, another overhaul is quietly under way. Republicans in Congress are attempting to remove healthcare insurance from under the aegis of employers and convert it into high-deductible "catastrophic" insurance workers would purchase that covers only the most severe health problems. Routine costs would be paid out of each individual's so-called "health savings account" – essentially, your own pocket with some tax sheltering added.

And for yet another example of how Republicans are stacking the environmental deck, The L.A.Times reports a survey in which more than 200 Fish and Wildlife researchers cited cases where conclusions were reversed to weaken protection for plants and animals and favor business. "The pressure to alter scientific reports for political reasons has become pervasive at Fish and Wildlife offices around the country, " said Lexi Shultz of the Union of Concerned Scientists. Take that, spotted owl! Take that, democratic process! It's good to be king.

George Duncan
Peterborough, NH

3.06.05

Keep 'em Barefoot and Ignorant

A column by former state senator Burt Cohen in the current issue of New Hampshire Business Review poses an interesting question: "Why are some pols afraid of teaching civics?" The "pols" he refers to are, of course, the Republicans in the State Legislature.

Cohen points out that although the Legislature's own 2002 study commission recommended that civics should be made a part of social studies education, the Republican majority stiffed it in 2003 and again in 2005. "What confuses and concerns me," says Cohen, "is why it's never Republicans who sponsor civics education bills. And even more baffling is why it's always the Republicans who actively work to defeat such measures." I would venture to guess that the savvy Mr. Cohen is being a bit facetious in his bafflement. But if he really wants an answer, it may be as obvious as it seems.

Republicans don't want young people growing up with a knowledge of their rights and of how democracy is supposed to work, so they can continue to run things the way they choose. Complete with Patriot Act assaults on the Constitution, distortion and duplicity in starting and prosecuting war, lies and smears in presidential campaigns, midnight ram rodding of bills, strong arm tactics and abuse of the rules in Congress itself and more. It has already been reported that high schoolers have little awareness of the first amendment. If the Republicans have their way, here in NH and elsewhere, the next generation of voters will be perfect dupes for the kind of myth making and cheap imagery that so heavily influenced the last election.

Politics may not be beanbag, as the saying famously goes, but in the United States, at least, it shouldn't be fascism, either.

George Duncan
Peterborough, NH

3.13.05

Sorry, Charlie

Last week I attended Congressman Charles Bass' Town Hall Meeting in Marlborough. There were about 150 people in the hall, with heavy representation from the Senior Class. As I entered, Charlie was trying to sound magnanimous in that he was keeping "an open mind" on Social Security matters. Probably a good move for this crowd which, it soon became apparent, was strongly opposed to private accounts, which Charlie supports. That open he isn't. He also made it clear at the outset that his answers to questions would be "policy" answers. In other words, he wasn't going to get into his personal views of issues raised which, I thought, was the purpose of the meeting. He had a handout with several pages of charts showing the usual money flows in and out of the system. I suspect most of the people there could have drawn them for him. As various speakers made it abundantly clear why they opposed private accounts, some adding thoughtful suggestions, Charlie nodded, even made notes, but I felt he wasn't really listening. Why? Maybe because this was his third such meeting and he had heard all this at the first two. He offered no proofs or even cogent arguments as to why he supports private accounts, except that his party told him to and he seems to think he can guarantee a risk-free market. No mention that the kinds of "safe" investments he suggests would yield minimal returns and add nothing to the system. No mention that private accounts are a zero-sum game; every dollar earned in an account is subtracted from the individual's regular Social Security benefit. Personally, I like Charlie. At heart, he's a good guy. But last Thursday, I am sorry to say, he left as he came. Still supporting the unsupportable. Still representing George Bush, not the people in that room.

George Duncan
Peterborough, NH

3.27.05

Bait and Switch

At Congressman Bass' recent Town Hall Meeting, and again in a letter to me from Senator Judd Gregg, I noticed an interesting bait and switch gambit. When speaking of the funds in which the so-called private accounts would be invested, (they suggest index funds) both Mr. Bass and Mr. Gregg are careful to emphasize the funds' safety. Then, to justify their enthusiasm for these accounts as saviors of the Social Security system, they promote images of a surging stock market. They exclaim that " the stock market has generated a real return (after inflation) of over 7 percent over the last 70 years," as Judd Gregg put it in his letter. But notice the switch from funds selected for safety to "the stock market" for high returns. As any investor knows, you can't have it both ways. The market operates on a risk-reward basis. The lower the risk, the lower the reward and vice-versa. For example, the largest of the index funds, Vanguard 500 Index, is returning MINUS 2.8% so far for 2005. The 5-year return is MINUS 3.4%! Further, even if you do make money in the private account, every dollar earned will be subtracted from the regular benefit, so if you think – as many do –that you'll be adding your private account profits to your regular benefit, forget it!

In Gregg's letter, he comments almost in passing, "while no one can predict the future…" Isn't that precisely the problem with Bush's privatization scam? That once you inject the stock market into the mix, any chance of guaranteed benefits go out the window? BUT, if we simply adjust the more familiar components as we have in the past – raise the salary cap (so Bush's buddies can share a bit more of the burden), increase the retirement age by a year or two, include a slight reduction in benefits phased in over 30 years, if necessary – we can have a risk-free guaranteed benefit just as we have always had.

According to the polls, the public is catching on to the Republicans' malarkey by 60% to 80% margins, depending on the poll. Notwithstanding the clear rejection of the privatization plan, Senate Finance Committee Chairman Charles A. Grassley told reporters he will continue to support them in the committee. "The president knows the first rule of politics is repetition," he said. So did Joseph Goebbels. Should we be fixing Social Security according to the rules of politics or the realities of economics? And do we really want policy by repetition?

George Duncan
Peterborough, NH

4.09.05

When arrogance becomes malignant

Having failed to place himself above God in the Terri Schiavo matter, Tom DeLay now wants to place himself above the federal courts. This guy is one of those radical conservatives -- my daughter calls them "Repugnants" or Repugs for short) -- who are driving our government, if not the country, over a right wing cliff. One of those who's arrogance transcends even partisan politics to become toxic and create, as with Nixon, a cancer at the seat of government.

The danger comes when Repugs like Bill Frist mistake Delay's media-driven infamy for license. Then they can do serious damage to the structures of government as with the so-called "nuclear option" to eliminate the 200-year-old filibuster rule. Frist is even cranking it up a notch by attempting to depict Democratic opposition to the policies espoused by a select few radical judges (out of more than 200 approved) as an attack on religion and fundamentalist beliefs. Most notably his beliefs. This self-righteous moral certitude with which the Repugs are now attempting to intimidate a constitutionally independent federal judiciary is nothing less than political pornography, in my view. A distortion of the political and moral dialog just as porn is a distortion of sex and with the same underlying power agenda.

Some say it would be the same if the Democrats ruled. Democrats did rule for forty years. Does anyone recall attacks on the institutions of government such as we are witnessing now? Attacks on privacy and on separation of Church and State? I don't think so. As economist John Kenneth Galbraith puts it, "The modern conservative is engaged in one of man's oldest exercises in moral philosophy; that is, the search for a superior moral justification for selfishness."

George Duncan
Peterborough, NH

4.17.05

The Subversives

In my early political experience, the Repuglicans were always the group most vociferously opposed to any activities they deemed "subversive" or "anti-American" throughout the 50's and 60's. Their zeal was personified by Senator Joseph McCarthy, a psychotic witch hunter and the poster boy for paranoid conservatives. What a surprise, therefore, to find that today it's the Repuglicans who are the subversives. First they subverted the truth about 9/11 by blurring the lines between Al Qaida and Iraq. Then they subverted the U.S. intelligence process by skewing the findings to support their pre-determined invasion of Iraq. Once the invasion was on, they subverted the U.S. military force structure by under-equipping our troops due to lack of intelligence. (The administration's ignorance of Iraq was then and still is stunning. Americans died because of it.) In prisons in both Iraq and Guantanamo, Kommandant Rumsfeld subverted the Geneva Convention with his torture protocols while here at home Reverend Ashcroft was busy subverting the Bill of Rights through the Patriot Act. Now we have Tom DeLay subverting the House Ethics Committee and Bill Frist subverting the Senate's time-honored filibuster rules in the name of God. Indeed, Frists' attempt to paint his Democratic opponents as being "against people of faith" is strongly reminiscent of those earlier anti-American witch hunts. If he succeeds in that characterization, we could well be witnessing the rise of a new McCarthyism.

George Duncan
Peterborough, NH

4.24.05

Fascism

In case you think "fascism" is too strong a word to apply to the Bush administration, get a load of this: The National Archives and Records Administration recently blocked a coalition of women's organizations from holding a Social Security forum at the Franklin D. Roosevelt Library in Hyde Park, N.Y., because the groups oppose Bush's private accounts. "If you cannot provide at least one speaker who will speak on the features and merits of the administration's plan for Social Security, then I must ask that you find another venue for your program," the library's director wrote to one of the groups sponsoring the forum. The library at the home of FDR -- who fathered the Social Security system 70 years ago -- is administered by the National Archives. And last month, two people were forcibly removed from a Bush event, simply because they had an anti-war sticker on their car.

Want more? The Bushies have decided that, to more thoroughly control the national dialog, they would produce their own news programs and foist them, unidentified as administration propaganda, on the public. You know, like Josef Goebbles did. And more recently, they discovered that their "Nuclear Option" – so named by Trent Lott – isn't polling well so they changed it to a more palatable "Constitutional Option." OK so far. But then they announced that any media outlet not using the new designation would be accused of demonstrating "liberal bias." The American Heritage Dictionary defines fascism as "Totalitarianism marked by right wing dictatorship and bellicose nationalism." It defines totalitarianism as, "…a form of government in which the political authority exercises absolute control over all aspects of life and opposition is outlawed." We may not be there just yet, but we need to pay attention.

George Duncan
Peterborough, NH

5.2.05

Cowards and Collaborators

Not surprisingly, the "smoking gun" memo leaked from Downing Street that proves the illegality of the Iraq invasion deal cut by Bush and Blair in July, 2002 has received almost no network or major cable TV coverage. There were articles in the L.A. Times and the Washington Post and several outraged pieces amongst the blogs and Web sites, but so far that's been it. Also, 90 Democratic Congressmen have signed a letter to Bush demanding an explanation. Fat chance, lacking any public outcry. Clearly, the corporate media – network and cable -- is laying low, afraid of Administration repercussions if they get too aggressive in their search for the truth. What's more, local stations around the country are actually using those video news releases the Administration is producing in support of Bush policies with no indication they're government propaganda. So our public media for the most part are either too cowardly to do their jobs, or collaborating with the government because they are ideologically in concert with the Bush agenda or hope to gain some financial or favor advantage. What was once a chorus of wackos – the so-called "blogosphere," is now the only place to get the truth. A few of these is Truthout.com, AlterNet.com, Fair.org and Arianna Huffington's new blog, Huffington Post.

"We're gutless. We're spineless. There's no joy in saying this, but beginning sometime in the 1980's, the American press by and large began to operate on the theory that the first order of business was to be popular with the person, organization, or institution that you cover." Dan Rather said that in 1991. He was ahead of this time.

George Duncan
Peterborough, NH

5.15.05

54

Outrages of the Week

The reason public broadcasting is coming under fire from right wing psychotics like Ann Coulter is that from the Ohio vote count to justifying the Iraq war to the death of Pat Tillman, this administration has lied about so much for so long that the truth is now seen as "biased." And, of course, anything that opposes Administration doctrine is "obstructionist." Sounding more like "Animal Farm" every day.

It speaks volumes of the Repug's respect for law and the democratic process when the Senate Majority Leader is prepared to trash more than 200 years of minority rights protection because he can't get his way. 204 judicial nominees confirmed out of 214 weren't enough – when the Republicans stymied more than 80 of Clinton's nominees and never let them out of committee. But Frist has to have it all because now he's in the majority so he's ready to stomp all over historic senate rules with his storm trooper boots.

Never mind that the Founding Fathers established Senatorial "advice and consent" precisely as a check against presidential power of which they were justifiably leery.

In the world, meanwhile, we've become the poster boy for the repression of human rights as regimes from Afghanistan to Zimbabwe take their cues from us. "When the most powerful country in the world thumbs its nose at the rule of law and human rights, it grants a license to others to commit abuse with impunity," Secretary General Irene Khan said in Amnesty International's 2005 annual report.

A Palestinian leader once described Chairman Arafat as "the rock we throw at the Israelis." The GOP, which has long wanted to do away with the UN entirely, now has a rock to throw at it – John Bolton. (And look at all that glass!).

George Duncan
Peterborough NH

6.3.05

What's In A Name? A lot!

During one of Congressman Charlie Bass' Town Meetings last March, he made reference on two occasions to what he called the "death tax." Each time he said it, a sizeable number of the people present quickly corrected him shouting, in unison, "inheritance tax!" Of course, it isn't difficult to understand why Charlie wouldn't want to remind the rest of us that this is, in fact, an inheritance tax – one that would fall on him and other wealthy elites like him. But the tactic is a typical right wing way of distorting the issues through language. Thus we have a "Clear Skies" program that pollutes the atmosphere, a "Safe Forests" initiative that opens old growth forests to logging, "No Child Left Behind" designed to destroy public education and, most recently, a "progressive benefits reduction" to Social Security. Sounds like "progressive taxation," doesn't it? But, failing in his effort to destroy Social Security through privatization, Bush is now trying to render it useless by cutting middle class benefits to the vanishing point. He knows, as well as Charlie Bass knows, that for wealthy people like them that Social Security check is chump change. They couldn't care less if their benefits are cut. But once middle class benefits are substantially reduced, Social Security becomes just another program for the poor, and highly vulnerable.

George Duncan
Peterborough, NH

6.12.05

The Visigoths of Governance

If you'd like a good example of how absolute power corrupts absolutely, take a trip to K Street in Washington, D.C. where many of the leading lobbyists are located. For better or for worse, lobbyists have enormous influence on legislation affecting everything from the pharmaceutical and entertainment industries to mutual funds, corporate governance and much more. During the 40 years that Democrats held the majority in Congress, executives of the Democratic persuasion and former Democratic officials naturally gravitated to these organizations over the years in a sort of organic growth. But now that Republicans hold sway, they are using the most blatant strong-arm tactics and what can only be described as extortion to force these lobby groups to fire the Democrats who have worked for them for years in many cases and hire Republicans. It's so organized, they even have a name for it: the "K-Street Project."

As a warning to other lobby groups, for example, Senator Sanctorum recently prodded House Republicans to remove from a pending bill $1.5 billion in tax relief for the motion picture industry, solely because the Motion Picture Association of America had hired a former Clinton cabinet official. Sanctorum, of course, prefers films that reflect his Christian sensibilities. From one end of K Street to the other, there are numerous reports of lobbyists being threatened with retribution and "lack of access" if they don't play ball. Talk about jack-booted thugs! These guys may dress better, but under their Joseph Abouds, they're the Visigoths of governance.

George Duncan
Peterborough, NH

6.19.05

58

The Ooops! Documents

The Terri Schiavo autopsy report is to Senators Frist and DeLay what the Downing Street Memo is to George Bush. That a doctor of Frist's stature could be so blinded by political expediency and so fooled by rabid ideology that he could violate every principle of medical ethics, let alone common sense, and presume to diagnose a person with so profound an illness -- a person he had never even examined -- on the strength of a videotape, indicates to me a dangerous man who has no place at the seat of democratic governance. DeLay's supreme arrogance, as Cyrano said of his nose, precedes him by half a mile. The man is a cartoon of greed, monetary and political. I don't know if it's a matter of conservatism so twisting the mind that its adherents simply become stupid or if the fear and paranoia on which conservatism is built eventually drives its victims nuts. Maybe Charlie Bass can tell us, since these are his mentors.

As for Mr. Bush and the Downing Street Memo, the (nonpartisan) Canadian Broadcasting Company reported: "Bush has always maintained that 'the use of force has been and remains our last resort.' But the memo could be the first documentary proof that Bush deceived the American people.

"During a forum organized by the U.S. House Judiciary Committee held to investigate the implications of the memo, Rep. John Conyers said the document 'means that more than 1,700 brave Americans and hundreds of thousands of innocent Iraqis would have lost their lives for a lie.'

"'It is a high crime to engage in a conspiracy to deceive and mislead the American people about the basis for taking the nation to war,' said constitutional lawyer John Bonifaz."

George Duncan
Peterborough, NH

6.18.05

Bush's PR War

Since early in 2002 when George Bush conspired with Britain's Tony Blair to invade Iraq and "fix the facts" around the policy, Bush, Cheney and the neocon cabal have been engaged in a PR war against the intelligence, goodwill and judgement of both Congress and the American people. As a result, we've had 1,731 US soldiers, 88 British soldiers and 93 from other nations killed since March 2003. An additional 13,000 troops have been wounded, many severely. An estimated 4,895 Iraqi soldiers and 22,507 civilians have been killed since the invasion. And for what? To shove Democracy down the throats of people who don't want it? To enrich Bush's petrocrat buddies? To satisfy the fantasies of some conservative think tank? Frankly, I don't really care what kind of government Iraq has. Let them have their civil war and work it out that way. It's up to them. Seems to me the only reason the insurgents are there is because we're there. And now, according to a recent CIA assessment, we've turned Iraq into the quintessential extremist training ground. Iraq is now what Afghanistan used to be – only better.

"The war has gone on longer and more violently than people envisioned," Sen. Lindsey O. Graham (R-S.C.) said. "People are dying in larger numbers than we thought, and the insurgency seems to be growing stronger, not weaker." Despite that sober – and rather obvious – assessment by a fellow Republican, the PR offensive continues with Bush e-nun-ci-a-ting to us all his treatise on war while Cheney intones that the insurgency is "in its last throes." He seems to be the only one who thinks so – except those whose careers he controls.

But what really offended me last week was Rumsfeld's comment at the Senate hearings about the loss of "coalition" soldiers. Almost as he spoke, 3 Marines were being killed by a suicide bomber and 3 more were missing.

U.S. Marines. Americans. Not "coalition" Marines. Those are American flags draping the coffins coming in to Dover AFB, not "coalition" flags. But because this is a PR war, Rumsfeld can't say "American." He can't afford to remind us that Americans are being killed. It would damage his PR.

George Duncan
Peterborough, NH

6.25.05

The Conservative Agenda

If you wonder whether the Republicans have long term goals for their current dominance of the Congress, you can't do better than a recent statement by Rep. Mike Pence (R-Ind.).

The Congressman said he and his colleagues will "fight to enact more tax cuts, pass spending curbs on entitlement programs such as Medicaid, impose new restrictions on abortion, get more conservative judges on the federal bench and increase the role of religion in public life."

In other words, Mr. Pence would shovel even more money into the pockets of the wealthy while further crippling the government's ability to respond to people's basic needs and "promote the general welfare." He would reduce the availability of health care for America's poor, limited as it already is. He would violate the privacy of women and inject his personal views into a choice that should rest solely between the individual, her family, and her healthcare and spiritual advisers. He would establish a conservative litmus test for admission to the federal bench (where decisions materially affect the lives of all Americans). And he would arrogantly and sanctimoniously seek to impose his personal religious views on the rest of us in violation of the recently reaffirmed constitutional principles of separation of church and state. (For examples of the confluence of church and state, see Iraq, Iran and Saudi Arabia.)

That's not governance in a democratic society. That's totalitarianism, and it has no place in America. It's also what you get when you have one party rule. What we need next year is not Social Security reform, or tax reform, or education reform, but Congressional reform.

George Duncan
Peterborough, NH

7.3.05

Darth Rove

Rep. Barney Frank, (D-MA.) urged Bush to "repudiate the destructive, dishonest assault" on liberals by Rove. "Karl Rove's vicious attack on people who have dared to disagree with the Bush administration policies consists primarily of conscious, deliberate lies," Frank said.

"Conservatives saw what happened to us on 9/11 and said: We will defeat our enemies. Liberals saw what happened to us and said: We must understand our enemies," he said. Sun Yat-sen, the famed "Father of the Chinese Revolution" once declared, "If you know the enemy and yourself, you need not fear the outcome of a hundred battles." We, apparently, know neither.

But more significant than Rove's words is the mind-set they convey. The "I'm the daddy and I'll tell you how to think" conservative world view that assures the radicals of their rectitude. It's a dangerous world, they believe (well, it is now) and they have been chosen to protect us – like they're protecting the Iraqis.

Now Rove is embroiled in the Valerie Plame matter. Apparently, he was the source of the petty, sophomoric "outing" of Joseph Wilson's wife, planting classified information in that worm Robert Novak's column as revenge for Wilson's refusal to follow the administration's bushwa around Iraq's supposed attempt to buy uranium in Niger.

Of course, it does no good to complain, because these people have no shame. Nor do they care about the legitimacy of their government. As Mark Morford put it in the San Francisco Examiner, "Lest you forget, this is what they do. They trim. They edit. They censor. Bush Co. kills what they do not like and fudges negative data where they see fit and completely rewrites whatever they want, and that includes bogus WMD reports and CIA investigations and dire environmental studies and scientific proofs about everything from evolution to abortion and pollution and clean air, right along with miserable unemployment data and all manner of research pointing up the ill health of the nation, the spirit, the world." And it's all done under Rove's watchful eye. A real class act, that guy.

George Duncan
Peterborough, NH 03458

7.10.05

75% in NH Oppose Private Accounts

Judging from the smoke signals emanating from the Congress, Bush's Social Security privatization plan may soon be raising its stupid head once again. This time, those of us in New Hampshire who oppose private accounts have something more than common sense to bring to the attention of our representatives – who, after all, have our best interests at heart, right? Right?

The University of New Hampshire Survey Center recently surveyed Granite Staters regarding the president's plan for Social Security. We're against it. And by hefty majorities. A few of the findings: 73% of those polled oppose creating private accounts if it requires the creation of a new government agency; 74% oppose creating private accounts that would change the way Social Security benefits are calculated; 77% oppose creating private accounts that require the federal government to borrow large sums of money; 60% agreed that Social Security "should remain a program that provides a predictable benefit without investment risk."

Apparently, though, the word hasn't filtered up (or is it down) to our representatives in Congress, who are sticking to Bush's privatization guns – even though he himself appears to be backing off – and the heck with what the rest of us think. That's representative democracy in a conservative administration where our "strict father" tells us what's best for us. It might help if more of us wrote, called or emailed our representatives to let them know what's best for them. You can access all four quickly and easily at; www.aarp.org/nh.

George Duncan
Peterborough, NH 03458

7.17.05

The King's New Clothes

Sure, now that one of their own is in jail, the press is making some noise about Rovegate. During the run-up to the war, any suggestion that maybe the Bushies were conning the American public was lucky to find a few inches on page 47. More "stuff" is coming out every day. Gonzales and the 12-hour gap. Colin Powell and the memo on Air Force One. And yes, even George Bush. Who said what to whom? By the time you read this, we may have our first "What did the president know and when did he know it?" comment. It's almost humorous that in his vindictive outing of Wilson's wife, Rove virtually confirmed the validity of Wilson's findings. Of course, Bush could clear the whole thing up in 30 minutes just by having everyone into the Oval Office and ask a few questions. But you and I know he'll never do that.

Perhaps Wilson said it best: "Clearly, the conspiracy to cover up the web of lies that underpinned the invasion of Iraq is more important to the White House than coming clean on a serious breach of national security….The real victims of this cover-up, which may have turned criminal, are the Congress, the Constitution and, most tragically, the Americans and Iraqis who have paid the ultimate price for Bush's folly." And the others who are still paying, he might have added, and will continue to pay in both lives and treasure, until a delegation of Republican Senators pays a visit to the White House and tells the king he indeed has no clothes…and there's a flight to Texas on the runway.

George Duncan
Peterborough, NH

7.27.05

68

Who's Your Daddy?

Following the defeat of Congressman Bass' scheme to create a trust fund for MBTE cleanups, he made a brief statement which I caught on NPR.

He said, despite the failure, he would continue to offer "new ideas." First, we should point out to Mr. Bass that shielding polluting energy corporations from lawsuits and passing the costs on to the taxpayers is, unfortunately, not a new idea. Neither is taking $14,000 from that champion of Texas energy companies, Tom DeLay.

He also said he was he was sent to Washington "to do a job" and to "make policy" and by gum, he's going to do it, irrespective of the opinions of others, was the gist. I assume the "others" includes those of us he represents who might have also thought it unwise to legislate away an individual's right to sue a polluter if he or she is harmed through their negligence. He doesn't seem to care much what we think about private accounts in Social Security, either. He clearly believes he knows better than we do what's in our best interest.

That's actually the conservative worldview, according to a book that's been raising eyebrows the last several months entitled "Don't Think of An Elephant" by George Lakoff (120 pages, $10 at the Toadstool). Lakoff, a linguist at U.C. Berkeley, shows how conservatives follow a "strict father" paradigm. It's a dangerous world, and it's up to them to dictate our behavior, for our own good, of course. The strict father is the moral authority who knows right from wrong and through strict discipline, can protect us from evil. Sound familiar?

The strict father model, says Lakoff, links discipline with the self-interested pursuit of success. Self-interest brings prosperity. Hence, conservatives oppose social programs that take care of people. Which might explain why, ., Congressman Bass voted to gut the NH laws that required health insurance companies to cover diabetic services – after taking $175,000 from heath insurance companies. Sure provides prosperity for him.

So when Charlie says he was sent to Washington to "do a job" and "make policy," watch out. Who's *your* daddy?

George Duncan
Peterborough, NH

8.2.05

The Late Show: How Charlie Bass, Tom DeLay and their Republican colleaguesare managing the people's business

It might be of interest to Peterborough voters to know how our good friend Charlie Bass, his good friend Tom DeLay and the Republican-controlled House have successfully passed several important bills this past year. In a recent article, Ohio Representative Sherrod Brown shed some light on what appears to be a very dark process, indeed.

"At 2:54 a.m. on a Friday in March," he begins, "the House cut veterans' benefits by three votes." This would have been around the anniversary of our troops' invasion of Iraq and of the arrival of the first American casualties.

At 2:39 a.m. on a Friday in April, Brown tells us, the House slashed education and health care by five votes. Leave no child behind, huh?

At 1:56 a.m. on a Friday in May, the House passed the tax-cut bill, weighted especially towards millionaires, by a handful of votes. Keep those checks coming in, guys.

At 2:33 a.m. on a Friday in June, the House passed the Medicare privatization bill by one vote. This bill effectively turns Medicare over to the HMOs.

At 12:57 a.m. on a Friday in June, the House eviscerated Head Start by one vote. Never mind the children left behind, let's keep them from getting started in the first place. And then, after returning from summer recess,

At 12:12 a.m. on a Friday . . . the House voted $87 billion for Iraq."

Note that each of these bills was passed, not only in the middle of the night, but on a Friday night, "Always after the press had passed their deadlines," says Rep. Brown. "At best," he continues, "Americans read a small story with a brief explanation of the bill and the vote count in the Saturday newspaper. And the Republican leadership knows that Saturday is the least-read newspaper of the week."

If this kind of thing bothers you, there is actually something you can do about it. This year, Charlie Bass is opposed for re-election by Paul Hodes, an "independent-minded Democrat" who points out that Charlie voted with the leadership 92% of the time. You'll find even more eye-opening Bass/DeLay abominations on Mr. Hodes web site, www.hodesforcongress.com/bass.html.

George Duncan
Peterborough, NH

12.29.05

2006

An excess of power

Seems like some Republicans just can't do anything in a straightforward, honest manner. They even scam their own! At the Republican straw poll in Memphis, an aide to Bill Frist went in to Nashville and brought busloads of supporters to the hotel. With the help of contributors, she paid the $150 registration for each so they could vote and ensure a First win in the straw poll!

And in a backroom deal announced last week, key Senate Republicans met with Dick Cheney and agreed to legislation that would rewrite our laws to require less disclosure and less judicial oversight of wiretaps than current law demands.

The message these partisans are sending to the people and the country is clear: Republicans are willing to put party loyalty over fundamental and timeless values, such as the preservation of the Constitution and the rightful power of Congress as a check on the president. Many Americans are appalled that Bush has not only ordered warrantless spying on Americans, but has unapologetically claimed that he has the power to break the law. "Where an excess of power prevails, property of no sort is duly respected. No man is safe in his opinions, his person, his faculties, or his possessions." -- James Madison

It's easy for Republicans to call for the Democrats to offer plans for the war or whatever when they know Democrats have no power in either house of Congress and can only stand by and watch while their proposals (including numerous bills) are shelved and ignored or the individuals involved swift-boated and trashed. When Senator Feingold dares to perform his sworn duty – to protect and defend the Constitution – and proposes a censure investigation of the President's abuses of that document, he's immediately labeled a "traitor." Garrison Keillor (D. Lake Wobegon), writes: "Democrats are accused of having no new ideas, but Republicans are making some of the old ideas look awfully good, such as constitutional checks and balances, fiscal responsibility, and the notion of realism in foreign affairs and taking actions that serve the national interest. What one might call 'conservatism.'"

I'm not crazy about the current inaction by so-called beltway Democrats, but the fact is, you don't plan for pools and patios while someone is trying to burn down the house.

George Duncan
Peterborough, NH

03.23.06

Beat the Press

Leave it to the Bush team to take a "shoot the messenger" approach to their problems in Iraq. As if the Shiites and Sunnis are killing and torturing each other so they'll get their names in U.S. newspapers. If there's so much great stuff going on in Iraq, why don't they show it to us? They're paying The Lincoln Group millions to plant feel-good bushwa in the Arab press, why don't they send some of that propaganda here so we can judge it for ourselves – along with their video press releases? Maybe the military is able to get to places the press can't. Which is just about anywhere outside the Green Zone.

An extensive article in the current New York Review describes, day by day, blow by blow, the difficulties facing journalists who are trying to cover the story there, whatever it is. Eighty-six journalists have died so far, trying to do just that. It's a bit difficult reporting on a school that may be operating somewhere, if you have to dodge a few car bombs to get to it. Reporters are no longer safe in Iraq. If they leave the Green Zone, their employers require they be accompanied by armed guards and travel at 90mph in armored SUV's, etc. Not exactly a typical news beat. The latest example is Jill Carroll, kidnapped and held captive for three months, her interpreter killed. She didn't have that armed guard protection, so she was fair game. That she wasn't killed is probably due to her expressed sympathies for the Iraqi people and the Christian Science Monitor's reputation as an honest interpreter of world cultures.

Speaking of Ms. Carroll, did you notice the instant hatred she drew from the brownshirts of trash radio? Because she made a statement opposing the war under the duress of captivity and a threat of death, and was shown in Muslim dress, and before they had any facts, these pea-brains immediately labeled her a traitor – salivating, I'm sure, for another Jane Fonda moment.

What a crowd. They spew their garbage to people who don't know or care about the truth of anything. Their sole purpose is to mine the anger of disaffected listeners in order gather an audience for advertisers. The sad part of it is, it works.

George Duncan
Peterborough, NH

04.06.06

Fool Me Twice

Fool me twice, shame on me. President Bush has certainly fooled us all more than twice. First, there was his cooking of the intelligence to create the illusion of a clear and present danger from Saddam Hussein in order to justify his pre-determined invasion of Iraq. Of this Paul Pillar, national intelligence officer for the Near East and South Asia at the CIA, writes in the March/April issue of Foreign Affairs: "Official intelligence analysis was not relied on in the decision to go to war; instead, selective intelligence was misused publicly to justify decisions already made."

Then came Bush's tap dancing around the FISA laws to conduct illegal electronic surveillance of U.S. citizens – after swearing that he always sought warrants. To keep us really safe, targets of the surveillance have included environmental groups (didn't know they were an enemy) and peace groups like the Quakers. Now there's this week's revelation that, in the words of The New York Times, "Mr. Bush, who has long criticized leaks of secret information as a threat to national security, himself approved Libby leaking just such information to the press in order to rebut a critic." The President may indeed have the legal authority to declassify information, but it isn't done on the fly. From my own time in Army Intelligence I know that there's a carefully detailed process for declassifying documents, including consulting the head of the agency involved - and the declassified documents are then distributed openly. As Representative Jane Harman, ranking Democrat on the House Intelligence Committee said, "Telling an aide to leak classified information to the New York Times is not a normal channel." And if the "declassification" was so above board, why did he stand there in front of cameras pretending to wonder who the leaker was? He said, "There are too many leaks of classified information in Washington….and if there is a leak out of my administration, I want to know who it is. And if the person has violated law, the person will be taken care of." Wow. Beats "I did not have sex with that woman…" all to heck, I'd say.

But the larger issue was articulated by John Dean: "A nation that cannot hold its commander-in-chief responsible is something other than a democracy."

George Duncan
Peterborough, NH

04.13.06

Charlie Bass

Republicans from Bush to Bass are throwing out everything in the standard conservative lexicon in the hope we won't notice that our government has been hijacked by a pack of criminals.

This election isn't about Charlie Bass, or about taxes as Charlie pathetically suggests. It's about the future of the country we live in and the country our children will live in. It's about "patriots" willing to sacrifice our young men and women's lives for a political agenda so nefarious, they have to lie about it. It's about the party of "family values" that quickly yield to political expediency. It's about sucking the economic vitality out of the middle class to further enrich the already rich, so they can return the favor. It's about power drunk cowards masking their evil deeds with hubris. And right here in our own backyard, we have Charlie Bass' policy director undermining our democratic election process with phony postings to the Internet in an effort to undercut his Democratic opponent, Paul Hodes.

Whether you like Charlie or not, he's irrelevant at best. He's made himself part of the problem, without a thought about the solution, other than more of the same. He offers no cogent reason to return him to Congress. Indeed, there's every reason not to, if you see and understand the abuses of the Constitution he and his party refuse even to recognize. If you're concerned about the war in Iraq and would like to see our soldiers out of the line of fire, you owe it to them to vote for change.

As Paul Hodes put it, "Charlie Bass is just a cog in a broken machine. He's a nice enough guy, but he's been ground up and spit out…When I go to Washington I'm bringing my backbone with me."

Democrats ran the House for more than 40 years and gave us most of the institutions that enrich our lives today from Social Security to Medicare and more. We can trust them to do it again. It's the only way to release the grip of this conservative cabal from throat of democracy and restore two-party balance to the House and Senate. Then perhaps, Republicans would be free to become Republicans again.

George Duncan
Peterborough, NH

10.12.06

Bush's judgment

George Bush said last week, "In my judgment," withdrawal from Iraq would mean surrender. But I think we know a few things about his judgment. It was his judgment to skew the intelligence findings from "we don't think so" to "there is no doubt" in creating the fabric of lies that justified his invasion of Iraq. It was his judgment that allowed Rumsfeld to play out his pet theory of minimal force at the continuing cost of American lives. It was his judgment to set up a network of secret prisons in foreign countries to do there what he could not legally do here. It was his judgment to permit the torture of "detainees" (everyone from terrorists to cab drivers) at Abu Graib and Guantanamo prisons, eliminate habeas corpus, deny legal representation and show the Iraqis that our justice system is the same as Saddam's.

It was his judgment to spy on American citizens illegally, to eavesdrop on our phone calls, collect our financial records and to arrogate to himself those and other powers not permitted under the U.S. Constitution—and then retroactively grant himself and his officials immunity from prosecution.

And now, with the highest death toll in two years in October and still no reliable electricity yet in Baghdad, it is his judgment that "we are winning" in Iraq. To paraphrase Winston Churchill, "Some winning. Some judgment."

George Duncan
Peterborough, NH

11-05-06

82

An end to the lies

So you really can't fool all of the people all of the time. Aside from the obscene squandering of life and treasure that is the Iraq debacle, my guess is the American people got tired of being lied to by their government. Every outright lie, every calculated exaggeration, every convoluted rationalization that Bush/Cheney/Rumsfeld foisted upon the electorate under the rubric of protecting us or "winning" in Iraq is an insult to our individual and collective intelligence. And when our elected representatives in the House and Senate either echo these monstrous assaults on our consciousness, or remain silent, they force us to act.

These are the people who, presumably, are of us. We sent them to Washington to speak for us, to act for us and while it is wise to avoid governance by opinion poll, there are equally good reasons to know what the people want from their government, especially in a time of war and crisis. Unless, like George Bush, you really don't give a damn.

One exposé after another revealed a cabal of opportunists seeking to profit by gaming the system. Often enough, these cretins model the bully-boy behavior of their leaders. One I love is the Republican penchant for referring to the Democratic Party as the "democrat" party. It's a form of school yard swagger intended to demonstrate their tough-guy disdain for the men and women who now represent at least half the voting public. Other examples include Senator Rick Sanctorum's "K-Street Project," designed to throw Democrats out of their jobs at the leading lobbying firms and replace them with Republican loyalists so they can funnel their client's money into party coffers. (Why do we need lobbyists? I forget.)

Bush can pretend to cooperate with Nancy Pelosi (of San Francisco!) all he wants. But, while we understand that politics ain't beanbag, we must not forget that these Republicans and their neocon cohorts have gone well beyond that. They have damaged America with their torture protocols, violations of U.S. and International law and the Constitution and more which they refuse to even acknowledge, let alone accept responsibility. You and I have a responsibility too, to tell our representatives what we want them to do – or not do – in our name. With Democrats now in power, there's a good chance we'll be heard.

George Duncan
Peterborough, NH

11-12-06

Democrats will share benefits

Attempting to draw a lesson from Vietnam, Bush complained last week that some, unfortunately, are looking for "instant success" in Iraq. Poor baby. He's just a victim of our unrealistic expectations. Never mind that it was he and his administration that sold Congress and the American people on instant success in the first place. So much so, that Rumsfeld made no plans beyond the fall of Baghdad. And since when is 3½ years "instant"?

Perhaps a better lesson of the Vietnam experience is don't lie to the American people about the progress of a war when their sons, daughters and husbands are giving their lives for it.

In true rats-from-a-sinking-ship style, the neocon morons who started all this are now attacking Bush for his incompetence in prosecuting the war. According to the Washington Post, Iraq war brain trust Kenneth Adelman says that "The failure to find weapons of mass destruction disturbed him." Pity. But that wasn't the failure. The failure was in insisting that Iraq was poised to attack us with WMD without a shred of solid evidence to back it up.

In the debate about exit strategies, Senator Carl Levin, soon to chair the Senate Armed Services Committee, has put forth a plan for phased withdrawal starting in four to six months. Cut and run? Not really. When asked in a Congressional hearing how long we have "to bring down the level of violence in Baghdad before it accelerates beyond control of even the Iraqi government," General Abizaid replied, "Four to six months." Is there an echo in here?

Ending the insanity in Iraq , improving life for middle class families, restoring our nation's civil liberties and judicial guarantees – these are some of the issues Democrats will address in the months ahead. And as Michael Moore writes in the L.A. Times (yes, that Michael Moore), Democrats will be happy to share the benefits of their policies with Republicans as well. E.J. Dionne wrote recently, "The British philosopher T.H. Green argued the 'ideal of true freedom is the maximum power for all the members of human society...to make the best of themselves.' This is not a bad description of the goals of the New Deal, the GI Bill, and the civil-rights movement." It's a pretty good goal for this Democratic Congress, too.

George Duncan
Peterborough, NH

11-19-06

Clarity on safety and torture

If there is one remaining reason why some still support the Bush administration, it's their promise to "keep us safe." Now comes a new National Intelligence Estimate, signed by all 16 intelligence services, that confirms what anyone with half a brain has been able to determine for themselves; that the war in Iraq is only increasing the terrorist threat, not reducing it, as the administration has claimed. Mind you, this report came out in April which means the president has been pushing the "safety" canard for five months now, knowing what that report said.

Can anyone tell us how "staying the course" in Iraq prevents any terrorist from a Timothy McVeigh to a Shoe Bomber from planting a bomb in an LNG tanker or blowing up the Lincoln Tunnel? Charlie Bass says we need to stay in Iraq until it "develops its own internal security to quell civil unrest." He doesn't suggest what we do if it doesn't. And it sure doesn't look like they're making much progress in that direction now. His rather naïve term "civil unrest' makes the sectarian civil war that's going on sound more like a bus strike. Then Charlie points to the fact that we still have troops in South Korea and Europe as though that were a good thing. As they say in the tuna ad, "Sorry, Charlie." One thing he did say that we can all agree with, "Two years from now the dynamics in Iraq will be completely different than what it is today." Well, du!

I was surprised and disappointed at John McCain's responses on "Face the Nation" to questions about his so-called compromise with the White House on the torture of prisoners. I thought he had a real deal. Turns out, he has no guarantees the administration will honor the agreement. His answer was, he takes Bush at his word. Hello? Maybe he doesn't read the newspapers either.

In a new report on human rights, the UN's Assistance Mission for Iraq says that torture is "still a widespread problem in official detention centers."

Bush says he seeks "clarity" around the issue of torture of prisoners and illegal detention. Intelligence was never the issue. What he's really seeking is permission to continue to ignore the laws and arrogate more power to himself.

George Duncan
Peterborough, NH

9.24.06

Let's vote for sanity

Some years ago, I was watching The McNeil-Lehrer Report on PBS. Rob McNeil was interviewing William F. Buckley, the foremost conservative thinker of these last 40 years. In response to a question, Buckley declared that he thought only college graduates should be allowed to vote. I thought McNeil was going to fall out of his chair. Not sure he had heard correctly, he asked Buckley to repeat it, which Buckley gladly did. That's the conservative view of equality. It was then, and it is now.

Indeed, in his new book, "Conservatives Without Conscience," former Nixon attorney John Dean looks at Republican-controlled Washington and sees a bullying, manipulative, prejudiced leadership edging the nation toward a dark era.

"Are we on the road to fascism?" he writes. "Clearly, we are not on that road yet. But it would not take much more misguided authoritarian leadership, or thoughtless following of such leaders, to find ourselves there."

I have often wondered why we elect to government people who don't believe in government? What kind of results do we expect? Will they "promote the general welfare" as promised in the Declaration and echoed twice in the Constitution? Interesting word, "promote." My dictionary says it means, "further the progress of; support or actively encourage."

To the contrary, as the Democratic Congressional Web site points out, "after 10 years of Republican control of Congress, House Republicans are determined to undo 74 years of Democratic accomplishments. The GOP wants to eliminate Social Security; privatize Medicare; dramatically scale back needed investments in education; ignore our national energy challenges; and open up our air and water systems to industry pollution and consumption for profit. And internationally, President Bush and the Republican leadership would have the United States "go it alone" in dangerous conflicts around the globe ignoring the small interconnected planet on which we all live.

We all see now, Democrat and Republican alike, where these policies have brought us. Do we need more? Read Democrat Paul Hodes' hopes and plans at www.hodesforcongress.com and let's vote for a return to sanity in November.

George Duncan
Peterborough, NH

Conspiracy of Abuse

It seems to me a poetic irony that the Bush Administration's latest initiative – the contract for Dubai Ports World – is falling victim to the administration's penchant for secrecy about everything it does, together with their refusal to inform Congressional leaders of their plans as out of the closet comes yet another secret committee. No doubt the Republicans will fall in line eventually and the deal will go through but the surprise was that despite the sensitivity of the port security issue, Bush didn't even know about it until after the fact. This is leadership? This is a war president?

But there is a much larger question at stake here. A "Bushwatch" blogger summarizes some of the abuses: in the Bush administration "the negation of truth has become systematic. Dishonest accounting, willful scientific illiteracy, bowdlerized federal fact sheets, payola paid to putative journalists, 'news' networks run by right-wing apparatchiks, think tanks devoted to propaganda rather than thought, a manufactured war, the purging of intelligence gatherers and experts throughout the bureaucracy whose findings might refute the party line, unauthorized surveillance of American citizens and opposition groups -- this is the machinery of mendacity."

The point here is not the hypocrisy involved, though that is egregious. The point is the downgrading of truth and honesty from principles with universal meaning to partisan weapons to be used or ignored as convenient. No wonder the Bush administration feels no compunction to honor the truth or seek it; it conceives truth as a tactic, valuable only insofar as it is useful against one's enemies. The American Prospect points out that while some abuses have existed in wartimes past, they were subsequently corrected as the threat passed. But "this president's conception of his own powers is even more dangerous than his specific abuses. This war promises to go on indefinitely – the so-called "long war." The threat then, is that these abuses of law and the Constitution will become a permanent part of our governance, especially with a conservative-leaning Supreme Court on hand to dismiss challenges. It's not just a matter of their conservatism, but rather their clear support for Bush's imperialist claims to power.

Saddest of all – and most dangerous – is the seeming acceptance by the general public of these violations their rights and the complicity of all too many of our so-called congressional representatives in the conspiracy. We must all vote in November.

George Duncan
Peterborough, NH

2.27.06

Cowards

Someone who knows finally said it out loud: The Bush Administration "cherry-picked" the intelligence on Iraq in order to promote a war they had long since decided upon. The man is Paul Pillar, a 28-year CIA veteran and the Deputy Chief of the Counterintelligence Center, responsible for coordinating all Iraq intelligence leading up to and following the invasion.

Had the administration been up front with the Congress and the American people and included the numerous warnings and caveats that came with the intelligence, there is little chance we would have kids dying in Iraq now. As for the Iraq-al Qaeda connection so definitively touted by Cheney, Mr. Pillar called it "manufactured."

Of course, it's been widely reported from numerous sources for years, Bush/ Cheney's denials, half-truths, untruths, distortions, etc., notwithstanding. but that's not the point. When I saw Cheney come out of hiding and run behind the skirts of Fox News to acknowledge the obvious, "I am responsible," (no kidding) it struck me as just another example of this administration's rank cowardice. These are clearly people who are afraid of having their ideas tested – or even discussed. It started with Bush's campaign appearances, always before hand-picked Republican minions where he could be assured of never getting a difficult question. It has continued up to today where he speaks only before large military audiences who must defer to him as Commander-in-Chief or before staunch Republican groups.

They stonewall the Congress and straight-arm the press – and indirectly, you and me – claiming confidentiality, secrecy, executive privilege, etc. for everything they do. Why? Because they know they're over the line and they're determined to keep it from us as long as they can.

When I use a word," Humpty Dumpty said, in a rather scornful tone, "it means just what I choose it to mean - neither more nor less." "The question is," said Alice, "whether you can make words mean so many different things." "The question is," said Humpty Dumpty, "which is to be master - that's all." -- Lewis Carroll: Through the Looking Glass.

George Duncan
Peterborough, NH

2.20.06

Epilogue

As indicated in my letter following the November 7th mid-term elections, it is encouraging, to say the least, to see that even this media-savvy administration failed to fool all of the people all of the time. But human beings, I believe, were created by our Higher Power to seek truth.

New Hampshire went totally Democratic at both the national and state levels with historic outcomes. Paul Hodes, whom I supported, beat Congressman Charles Bass both in the district and, amazingly, here in Peterborough, Mr. Bass' home town. I sincerely hope my letters played some small role in that.

If anything, the Republican and neocon manipulation of the media these past six years should be a cautionary tale for all of us going forward. In that regard I would urge progressives to read bloggers Jerome Armstrong (MyDD. com)and Markos Moulitsas Zuniga's (Daily Kos.com) book, "Crashing the Gate" (www.chelseagreen.com). I look forward to their responses to the election, now that the netroots and grassroots have spoken. I have added a suggested bibliography below.

The challenge now will be to sustain the proactive stance that helped lead us to victory. George Bush, after all, is still president, and his consigliore, Cheney, is still running the show. John McCain's candidacy remains a serious threat to whatever gains we may enjoy between now and 2008, and there are other "conrads" (conservative radicals) with designs on the White House.

Those of us who may not be directly connected to campaigns or policy groups need to inform ourselves of the issues – and even more importantly of the people who will presume to lead us in the future. We must ask who is this person? What has he or she done in their lives? What do they read?

What have they written? What do friends and opponents say of them? And this time we should not ignore what we know – as we did with Bush.

The enemy here is not the Republican Party. On any level playing field, the nurturant philosophies of Liberalism will always win out over the repressive dictates of conservatism. Democrats seek programs and policies that follow the Constitutional mandate to "promote the general welfare" and we always will. Note the word "promote." Not "support" or "assist" or "observe." Promotion is a proactive process. It requires a smoothly functioning government. Republicans oppose government of any kind. And yet we keep electing them to public office. Probably because a skillful media blitz can fool some of the people some of the time.

In my opinion, no Republican administration has ever proposed a policy or program that has benefited the American public at large. Theirs is a preventive stance. A withholding philosophy. The Doctor No of politics. A diminution of life, liberty and pursuit of happiness, often disguised as individual liberty. But man was made a social animal who builds societies for mutual support and protection. And we are blessed to be living in the greatest social experiment in history. Thus Democrats have given us the assurances and protections of The New Deal, Social Security, civil rights and the equalities of The Great Society, worker's rights, women's rights, Medicare, unemployment insurance, The Family and Medical leave Act, the minimum wage. All these and more are part of the social contract to promote the general welfare and all were vigorously opposed by Republicans.

Further, conservatism is routinely marked by racial and religious intolerance, bigotry towards gays and misogyny towards women. It shows contempt for the poor and disadvantaged and it's militaristic, projecting an ugly authoritarianism well described by John Dean in his book.

George Duncan
Peterborough, NH

12.03.06

96

Felonious Speech?

Over the years, Americans of both parties have huffed and puffed at the control of the press by such repressive regimes as North Korea and Communist China, expressing understandable pride for the freedoms of speech and the press we enjoy here. So it may surprise you to learn -- at this late date -- that this past April, President Bush was prevented from speaking at Stanford University by a student demonstration. Yes, successfully prevented. That certainly should have made some headlines, but it didn't. No press coverage of any significance, save a piece in the April 24 Stanford Daily. Which suggests a control of the press by this administration of which few of us were aware.

And if that doesn't give you a chill, try this. Jim Hightower reports that there's a new felony abroad in the land: the constitutional rights we used to call Freedom of Speech and Freedom of Assembly have been compromised by a provision of the Patriot Act that authorizes the Secret Service to charge suspects with breaching security or disruptive behavior at "National Special Security Events." That's anywhere the President or other protected person happens to be, even temporarily; speech, rally, the Olympics, ball park, etc. Or any place the President risks proximity to someone who opposes his policies. This turns what might have been a trespassing misdemeanor into a felony. We've seen people removed or detained for wearing the wrong T-shirt or having an anti-Bush bumper sticker. Now you can be held for saying the wrong thing. You know, like in North Korea and Communist China.

George Duncan
Peterborough

7.11.06

Bush bashing: the Rovian response

In a letter to the editor last week, the writer, clearly of the conservative persuasion, referred to the various criticisms of Bush administration policies as "Bush bashing." This is a junior version of Karl Rove's slick tactic of dismissing legitimate criticism as politically motivated vitriol and then sliming the critic as though that somehow changes the facts. It also substitutes in today's media for anything resembling a reasoned response. It's a method that allows the Bushies to pretend that, any critique of the president's behavior is just politics-as-usual and should be ignored.

The litany of Bush's missteps and deliberate abuses of U.S. and international law has grown too long and too grievous to be ignored by any thinking citizen, regardless of party. The polls tell us that there will always be that 30% who are too uninformed or unconcerned to think anything through for themselves, but the rest of us have a responsibility to call a spade a spade and do what we can to protect our country and our Constitution, not to mention our reputation in the world. Those who have sworn an oath to that effect, of course, are obligated to do so. Frankly, Bush the man is too insignificant to spend time and effort bashing. Bush the president, however, is another matter. He is a danger to all of us and to our children as well and we must speak out.

"That we are to stand by the president, right or wrong is not only unpatriotic and servile, but is morally treasonable to the American public." -- *Theodore Roosevelt*

George Duncan
Peterborough, NH

11.24.06

98

Bush's tortuous clarity

Speaking in support of his torturous interrogation program, George Bush said, "If not for this program, our intelligence community believes al Qaida and its allies would have succeeded in launching another attack against the American homeland." Though it pains me to say it, I don't believe him. He has shown himself willing to say whatever he needs to say to advance his personal agenda even at the cost of innocent life. He and Cheney have also proven themselves quite capable of either mis-representing the findings of the intelligence community, or of intimidating them into "finding" what they want them to find.

Newsweek's Evan Thomas has his doubts too. "In recent interviews with Newsweek reporters, U.S. intelligence officers say they have little - if any - evidence that useful intelligence has been obtained using techniques generally understood to be torture."

Fact is, The Financial Times reports, "The Bush administration had to empty its secret prisons and transfer terror suspects to the military-run detention centre at Guantánamo this month in part because CIA interrogators had refused to carry out further interrogations and run the secret facilities, according to former CIA officials and people close to the programme." So much for essential intelligence.

Bush says he seeks "clarity" around the issue of torture of prisoners and illegal detention. (Whatever happened to training?). What he's really seeking is permission to ignore the law.

A Buzzflash.com editorial puts it well, I think: "For more years than we can remember, the Geneva Convention has guided the conduct of civilized nations in matters of war. America has abided by the treaty without dissent or difficulty. In fact, we prided ourselves on implementing the standards spelled out by the Geneva Convention for the treatment of prisoners of war. But Bush is now saying, that suddenly for him, the Geneva Conventions do not provide 'clarity.' This, of course, is the use of framing to make a betrayal of the American people by the Bush Administration look like a reasonable act. The Geneva Conventions have provided uncontested 'clarity' through multiple Republican and Democratic administrations, but all of a sudden they have become 'vague' to Bush, even though not a word in them has been changed."

Fact is, "intelligence" was never the issue. Bypassing the laws and arrogating more power to himself, is.

George Duncan
Peterborough, NH

9.16.06

Charlie, we hardly knew you

Any doubt that Charlie Bass is firmly entrenched in the conservative thugocracy was removed last week when his policy director – not some irresponsible grunt, mind you, but a top advisor – posted a series of "dirty trick" messages on the Internet, posing as a Paul Hodes supporter, but belittling his campaign.

My first reaction was that this was such a low-end, but typically Republican trick that it should have been beneath the Charlie Bass I used to know. Obviously, however, it wasn't. Then I felt violated by the nerve of some jerk thinking he could pull this on me.

I hope Charlie apologizes directly to Paul and to all of us who plan to vote in November, and the jerk goes to jail as his previous colleague did in the phone tampering stunt last election. It simply reinforces the disdain that some conservatives have for the election process – just too democratic for them, like William F. Buckley suggesting that only college graduates should be allowed to vote. Why, I keep asking, do we put people into government who do not believe in government?

Then Charlie drops the other dirty shoe – running a "swift boat" type ad mis-stating Paul Hodes' position on Iraq. Charlie says Paul wants to send U.S. troops to "Kurdestan." Oooo. Sounds like Russia, doesn't it? Does he really think we're all too stupid to know that Kurdestan is what the Kurds call Northern Iraq? And that if we were to re-deploy away from the heavily insurgent areas as has been suggested (not by Paul Hodes, but by others), Northern Iraq is undoubtedly one of the places we'd go?

Further, anyone who wants to know Paul Hodes' position on Iraq can read it for themselves on his web site at www.hodesforcongress.com. Try it. I think you'll find it quite reasoned – given the fact that, thanks to Bush's total incompetence, there are no good choices in Iraq.

On June 28, 2004, Condi Rice passed a note to President Bush as Ambassador Bremers plane left Baghdad: "Iraq is sovereign..." Really? Then what are we doing there? We should take a tip from a NY Times letter writer and let the Iraqis vote on whether we stay or go. A recent poll suggests that 75% of Iraqis now want us out.

Charlie also voted for Bush's torture and detention policy, by the way.

George Duncan
Peterborough, NH

9.29.06

Climate of Fear

As President Bush scrambles to negotiate something resembling rights for the detainees in Guantanamo following the Supreme Court's rebuke of his anti-Geneva Convention and generally unconstitutional agenda, Republican Texas Congressman Ron Paul said the following: "I would have trouble arguing that he's been a Constitutional President, and once you violate the Constitution and be proven to do that I think these people should be removed from office."

And this: "Congress has generously ignored the Constitution while the President flaunts it, the courts have ignored it and they get in the business of legislating so there's no respect for the rule of law."

And this: "When the President signs all these bills and then adds statements after saying I have no intention of following it - he's in a way signing it and vetoing - so in his mind he's vetoing a lot of bills, in our mind under the rule of law he hasn't vetoed a thing."

And Paul said the United States had entered a period of "soft fascism."

This is a Republican Congressman saying this. And yet we have our own Republican Congressman defending this President in the face of what any sentient being would have to conclude are serious abuses of the very Constitutional laws he has sworn to uphold.

Bush/Cheney have worked long and hard to maintain a climate of fear in America, throwing the images of 9/11 in our faces at every turn and using it to co-opt the Congress and build a power center in the White House. And now Newt Gingrich, in what may be a preview of Republican election strategy, is running around the country saying we're in World War III.

All totalitarian regimes have used fear as a form of mind control, from Mao to Saddam. (Know why Bush won't engage North Korea in the one-on-one talks which they seek? Because John Kerry suggested exactly that in the campaign debate and Bush ridiculed him for it.) Bush knows the longer he can keep that ball the air – along with Iraq and Al Qaeda – the longer he can hold the specter of fear over the voters' heads.

This November let's not vote our fears, but our consciences. Fears come and go. Our consciences are with us always.

George Duncan
Peterborough, NH

7.15.06

The Right-Wing at OMB

During the Clinton administration, Hillary was hooted down when she made accusations of a "vast right-wing conspiracy" that she thought was targeting her and the President. Whether you choose to call it a conspiracy or not, there is clearly a vast conservative movement afoot which is gradually taking over the mechanisms of government and replacing experienced, qualified professionals with political apparatchiks whose only goal is to gut long established policies and programs and government regulation generally. Here's just one example.

The Office of Information and Regulatory Affairs at OMB (Office of Management and Budget) approves all environmental, health and safety and other government regulations.

According to Al Kamen at the Washington Post, Bush's nominee to head this office is Susan Dudley, who is currently director of the regulatory studies program at George Mason University's Mercatus Center.

The Mercatus Center is largely funded, says Kamen, by Koch Industries Inc., the oil and gas company and mega-GOP contributor. *Charles G. Koch* and another top Koch (pronounced "coke,") official serve on the nine-member Mercatus board of directors. According to the Center for Public Integrity, Koch money controls or strongly influences a number of leading conservative institutions, including the Cato Institute (co-founded by Charles Koch), the Tax Foundation, the Institute for Justice, the Federalist Society, and Citizens for a Sound Economy, which was founded in 1984 by Charles and David Koch and another Koch executive.

"Dudley," says Kamen, "would seem to be the obvious successor to continue the administration's anti-regulatory policies. In the early days of

President Bush's first term, when the OMB asked for public input on which regulations should be revised or killed, Mercatus submitted 44 of the 71 proposals the OMB received. And the OMB approved 15 of them. These recommendations critiqued onerous regulations such as that silly EPA rule limiting the amount of arsenic in drinking water. (Hey! You don't want it? Don't drink it.)"

In other words, Dudley would set about ignoring and even killing regulations designed to protect our air, national parks, workplace safety and more. An example of the conservative approach to bureaucracy with major consequences for the American people. And it's being repeated every day throughout government.

We could begin to reverse abuses like this by voting Democratic in November and restoring some balance to the Congress.

George Duncan
Peterborough, NH

7.30.06

Contempt for Governance

Declaring Bush the flat-out worst president in American history, a cover story in Rolling Stone by Princeton historian and Pulitzer Prize-winning author Sean Wilentz, listed the now familiar litany of Bush Administration outrages: the war, the wrecked economy, the deficit, Katrina, Plamegate, fundamentalist hostility to science and subversion of the Constitution. To that we could add the Administration's global warming cop-out, manipulation of pre-9/11 intelligence, and in broader terms, Bush's appalling moral leadership: the lies and self-serving leaks, the reckless doctrine of pre-emptive war and, maybe most of all, the introduction of torture as a fixture of U.S. military policy.

The word we often hear in connection with these issues is "incompetence."

Certainly, we had no good reason to expect better, given Bush's unbroken record of failures prior to election. He was loser at Yale, he blew his flight status in the Texas Air National Guard, he drove an oil company close to bankruptcy and played fast and loose with a baseball team. He was so obviously challenged that his intelligence, or lack thereof, became the source of numerous gags in the months leading up to the election. Despite all that, however, I think the issue with Bush and his cohorts is more serious than mere incompetence. I think, deep in his inner self, he harbors raw contempt for ordinary people and for the processes of democratic, Constitutional governance.

George Duncan
Peterborough, NH

5.19.06

2007

PORTRAITS & AUTOGRAPHS OF THE SIGNERS OF THE DECLARATION OF INDEPENDENCE.

Patriot Games

"U.N. calls U.S. data on Iran's nuclear aims unreliable. Tips about supposed secret weapons sites and documents with missile designs haven't panned out, diplomats say." So reads a headline in the NY Times as Bush & Company try to distract our attention from their failures in Iraq by pushing the War President's agenda into Iran. Naturally, it just reminds us of the phony intelligence reports that led to the Iraq war, and the consequences of a presidency that's out of control. The Pentagon inspector general just issued a devastating report describing how Cheney's agents in the Defense Department distorted intelligence to "prove" the mythical linkage between Osama bin Laden and Saddam Hussein. Nevertheless, Cheney has clearly stated it makes no difference what anyone thinks, they're going ahead with their plans, because they know best – and who's to stop them? To get any meaningful traction for a countermeasure requires 60 votes to halt a Republican filibuster and there are still enough dead enders in the Senate more loyal to the President and the party than to the American people.

Peter Galbraith has a devastating analysis of Bush's so-called "surge" in the current NY Review. He concludes, "George W. Bush has said he will leave the problem of Iraq to the president elected in 2008. Rather than acknowledge failure in Iraq – and by extension a failed presidency – Bush has chosen to postpone the day of reckoning. It is a decision that will cost many American and Iraqi lives, will leave the United States weaker, and will prolong the decline in American prestige abroad caused by the mismanaged Iraq war. And it will not change the truth that the President so desperately wishes to escape: George W. Bush launched and lost America's Iraq war."

Regarding Iran, Karen Kwiatkowski, a retired Air Force Lieutenant Colonel formerly with the National Security Agency, points out that the main thrust for war with Iran is coming from the Air Force and the Navy – the two services that were left out of Iraq…twice. Interesting point. And not a surprise, given the inter-agency competition at the higher levels where budgets and appropriations are made. We don't plan to invade Iran but that doesn't mean we can't attack from the safer distances of B-1 bombers and aircraft carrier groups. I guess it all depends on what the meaning of "invade" is.

George Duncan
Peterborough, NH

03.08.07

Bush-Rove-Cheney and the Conservatives' Police State

It's becoming clearer that Bush, Rove & Co. saw an opportunity to use the system of federal prosecutors as their secret private police to pursue Democrats and ease off on cases where Republicans and/or their corporate supporters were subjects of investigations. As The Nation put it, "This White House views these attorneys not as law-enforcement professionals but as partisan muscle for its entwined political and policy ambitions."

Foremost among those ambitions was Karl Rove's stated purpose to create "a permanent Republican majority." Imagine what that means in a pluralistic, democratic, two-party system where, in the 2000 and 2004 elections voters were evenly divided and in 2006, according to CNN/USA Today/Gallup, 49% voted Democratic and 43% voted Republican. For Rove's policy to succeed, methods must be devised to circumvent or destroy existing institutions and processes and this manipulation of the U.S. attorneys is a good example. After 9/11 almost anything could be explained away under cover of protecting the American people, like the Patriot Act that allows Bush to bypass the Congress in making U.S. attorney appointments. Or the prostitution of the CIA and FBI, using them to eavesdrop on U.S. citizens and examine their finances by virtue of Alberto Gonzales' interpretation of the Constitution.

Now we see that The Republican National Committee deployed officers of the New York City police department as undercover spies who, for at least a year before the 2004 Republican National Convention, went around the country attending meetings of political groups, posing as sympathizers or fellow activists and collecting information on anti-war and other perfectly legal organizations. So apparently any city's police department can be turned into an intelligence arm of the Republican party?

Somehow, we must find a way to end this secret, creeping militarization of our country.

George Duncan
Peterborough, NH

03.29.07

Leave Bush Alone

I wish the Democrats would leave President Bush alone. The press and the pundits, too. And I mean all alone. No press conferences, no public appearances, no speeches, no helicopters on the South Lawn, no cameras. Let him sign or veto bills in the Oval Office by himself. Move the Cabinet to the Executive Office Building. He and Rove and the guy with the codes can wander around anywhere they like on the White House grounds. And that's it.

Maybe when the troops are back home, when the work crews have restored the damage from Katrina, when Condi has deals with Iran, Syria, North Korea and China, when Cheney has resigned and is back in Texas killing little birds – if not in jail – then maybe Bush could be allowed to apologize to the American people and to the service families and slink back to Crawford.

This idea was dramatically underscored by a film clip a friend discovered on Utube and sent to me. It was of a recent Bush press conference – one we'll probably not hear much about. At the conclusion of his statements, Bush asked, as per usual, for questions. There were none. Bush pointed to this reporter, then that one, then another. In each case the reporter sat in deafening stonefaced silence until Bush got the message, said thank you and left. After all, when you know you're talking to a liar, why ask questions? Here's the link: www.utube.com/watch?v=qdRUgXxCOeU.

The other people who need to be dealt with in similar fashion are the neocons whose arrogant grab for world power got us into this mess in the first place. Sounds like a plot from a comic book, doesn't it? A dozen Penquins plotting to control the world, and no Bat Man in sight. Most of them are members of the American Enterprise Institute, a so-called "think tank" that has to be the snake pit of the universe. Their plan was called the Project for the New American Century. It's couched in the delicate verbiage of diplomacy, to be sure, but it's pure arrogance with a dollop of schoolyard bully.

It's signed by Elliott Abrams, Gary Bauer, William Bennett, Jeb Bush, Donald Kagan (author of the "surge"), Cheney, Libby, Rumsfeld, Wolfowitz and others. You'll find them at www.newamericancentury.org/statementofprinciples.htm. These people should also be shunned and never allowed to work in government again.

George Duncan
Peterborough, NH

03.15.07

Some conservatives finally get it

Bruce Fein served as associate deputy attorney general under President Ronald Reagan and is a founder of a conservative movement known as the Liberty Coalition. As reported on Truthout.com earlier this month, the Coalition has launched a new initiative, known as the American Freedom Agenda. Among its primary goals is a call upon Congress to restore checks and balances within the government and rein in the power of President George W. Bush.

They list ten specific abuses they want to see addressed. They include, end the use of military commissions to prosecute crimes; prohibit the use of secret evidence or evidence obtained by torture; prohibit the detention of American citizens as enemy combatants without proof; restore habeas corpus for alleged alien combatants; end National Security Agency warrantless wiretapping; challenge presidential signing statements, bar executive use of the state-secret privilege to deny justice; prohibit the president from collaborating with foreign governments to kidnap, detain or torture persons abroad; amend the Espionage Act to permit journalists to report on classified national security matters without threat of persecution; prohibit of the labeling of groups or individuals in the US as global terrorists based on secret evidence.

It's refreshing to see conservatives take steps – or appear to do so – to reverse some of the Bush Administration's overreaching violations of the Constitution – after, of course, Mr. Rove took care to re-interpret it to his purposes. I'm willing to park my cynicism a while to see if anything comes of it. But two points can be made. First, it's by no means a definitive list. At best it's a good start. Second, it amounts to a list of failures by the recent rubber stamp, Republican-controlled Congress to speak out against these abuses and others in the name of Bush loyalty and conservative ideology, which was more important than the Constitution or the rights of the people.

Two such Senators still represent New Hampshire and one is up for re-election next November. These ten points are among the questions we need to ask any Republican running for office until such time as the Republican Party publicly disavows this kind of thuggery in government.

George Duncan
Peterborough, NH

04.31.07

Profiles in Cowardice

Paul Wolfowitz wasn't forced to resign his World Bank payoff job because he arranged a raise for his girlfriend. That was just the excuse. Wolfowitz was so universally disliked by the Bank staff, they were delighted to seize on anything they could to get him out of there. Fortunately, he tripped over his own arrogance and provided them an opportunity. Wolfowitz came into his Bank sinecure already distrusting everyone in the place and determined to run things his way, with his own people – political hacks who pushed out the more competent professionals.

If it were an isolated incident, it wouldn't be worth a lot of attention, notwithstanding Wolfowitz being a prime architect of the Iraq war. But the Wolfowitz debacle is just part of a larger trend in this conservative administration, and you and I need to pay attention to it if we're going to restore integrity and competence to our government agencies.

John Bolton went to his UN post with much the same attitudes.

And Rumsfeld at Defense ignored experienced Pentagon professionals, both military and intelligence, to replace their wisdom with his own ego. We're still seeing the results in Iraq every day.

At the Attorney General's slot, first John Ashcroft violated the Constitution between prayer meetings with his repugnant Patriot Act, then Bush boot licker Alberto Gonzales keeps forgetting how he tried to turn the department into Karl Rove's political play pen.

At the CIA, George Tenet who, as Ray McGovern says, "could not muster the integrity simply to tell the truth and stave off unspeakable carnage in

Iraq", willingly accepted the "Presidential Medal of Silence" before resigning to write a pathetic *apologia pro sua vita*.

But why should we be surprised when, at the apex of this Profile in Cowardice is George Bush who, as President, has systematically scoffed at the Constitution and worked feverishly to replace competent, experienced professionals with "loyal" political cronies in department after department. The result is that today most regulatory agencies are headed by former lobbyists or executives from the industries they're supposed to regulate.

Instead of presidential candidates telling us how they'll bring us all together, we'd be better served by their views of Bush's "unitary executive" concept, habeas corpus, torture of prisoners, warrantless wiretapping, presidential signing statements and other abuses of this administration. Let's not let it happen again.

George Duncan
Peterborough, NH

05.24.07

The true pain of Memorial Day is Bush's intransigence

From the White House to the Town House, CNN to NPR, the memorials for the fallen and the celebrations of the bravely wounded working so hard to carry on were especially painful this year when one realizes it is all for no practical result, except to salve the egos of a diminishing handful of conservative politicians hiding behind the shibboleths of patriotism.

Rory Stewart is a former member of the British Foreign Office who from 2003 to 2004 was the Coalition Provisional Authority's Deputy Governor in the southern provinces of Iraq. His comments, published in The New York Review, are especially knowledgeable, and much in concert with other non-partisan observers of the situation now in Iraq. "I believe that the time has come to withdraw, that our presence is infantilizing the Iraqi political system. That we're like an inadequate antibiotic; sufficiently strong to have turned what might have been a conventional civil war into a highly unconventional neighborhood conflict, but not strong enough to eliminate it entirely. At the same time I fear that, without intending to, we have discredited democracy in the eyes of many Iraqis. We have created a situation in which many Iraqis now feel the only way to keep security is to bring back a strongman. They are extremely skeptical of our programs and suggestions for development.

"Whatever government emerges after our departure is likely to be Islamist and authoritarian. Despite some claims to the contrary, there is not a single indicator of significant, overall improvement I know of over the last four years, neither in electricity, nor in education, nor in police training, nor in the military. There is no evidence I have seen that either the Iraqi police or army is prepared to take over our role, so long as we stay. Starting to leave tomorrow as opposed to two years' time or six years' time would make no difference; the situation would be the same. And there can be no justification for continuing, day by day, to kill Iraqis and to have our own soldiers killed in this kind of war."

I can only pray that such patently obvious common sense will soon overcome the hubris of our leaders and allow our brave troops – the true patriots – to stand down from Bush's ignorant, reckless war.

George Duncan
Peterborough, NH

05.31.07

"Keep your poor…"

So from the debates, we see the clear choice. If you believe the U.S. should reserve the right to unilaterally attack any country that's not a democracy and force the U.S. Constitution down their throats, vote Republican. (Question: would that be George Bush's Constitution, or the original?) But if you believe that the best way to support our troops is by getting them out of harm's way in what has deteriorated into an ethnic cleansing Iraqi civil war, vote Democratic. In the debates, the Republicans to a man supported the surge and supported the war. Republicans, of course, dislike poor management and while some were willing to acknowledge the war has been "mis-managed," not one of these stalwarts questioned the premise upon which the war was foisted upon the American and Iraqi people through ignoring and manipulating the intelligence, innuendo, outright lies and unremitting fear-based rhetoric. Now as the Iraq debacle comes crashing down around their heads, they obviously have to change the subject.

So let's see, what's this? We're shocked-shocked to discover illegal aliens in the U.S.! Here's a target we can beat–the poorest, least powerful people in the country. Mostly Mexicans who for almost 15 years have been coming over the border to find work in the U.S. as house cleaners, maids and waitresses, pot wallopers in hotel kitchens, car wash attendants, gardeners, farm laborers, etc. (Question: If those jobs are so sought after by Americans, why are they available?) What started this migration? Last week, "Granny D" spoke at an event in Bedford. There she drew a clear, bright line from the present influx of "unauthorized" immigrants (she refused to call them "illegal aliens") to the passage of NAFTA. NAFTA gave U.S. Agri-giants access to Mexican markets which soon drove more than half of Mexico's farmers into bankruptcy, putting thousands out of work.

For more than two hundred years we've welcomed immigrants to this country and worked out accommodations for their entry. But those were European immigrants. They looked like us. These people are…brown. Seems to me when you have a law that's been routinely ignored by the people and by the enforcement agencies to the tune of more than 12 million people over 15 years, it's time look at the law, not the people. And if our law-and order Republicans want to enforce the laws, let them start with the White House.

George Duncan
Peterborough, NH

06.14.07

Defend the Constitution

On July 4th, I had the privilege of reading the Declaration of Independence at the Historical Society's annual observance of Independence Day. There were a few children in the audience, but not nearly enough, in my view. Our young people especially need to understand the principles this country was founded upon, since they are the ones who will carry them forward. Or not. The previous Sunday, historian/author Howard Zinn wrote in the New York Times, "I want young people to understand that ours is a beautiful country, but it has been taken over by men who have no respect for human rights or constitutional liberties. Our people are basically decent and caring, and our highest ideals are expressed in the Declaration of Independence which says that all of us have an equal right to 'life, liberty and the pursuit of happiness.' The history of our country is a striving, against corporate robber barons and war makers, to make those ideals a reality – and all of us, whatever age, can find immense satisfaction in becoming part of that."

When I was commissioned in the Army many years ago, I took an oath to "preserve, protect and defend the Constitution against all enemies, foreign and domestic."It's an oath I consider to be still in effect. Today our Constitution is under attack from domestic enemies and we all have a responsibility to defend it, with or without a formal oath. The best way to do that, I think, is first to inform ourselves of the nature of the attack and then to use our constitutionally guaranteed vote to remove those who support the enemies of our Constitution and to hold those who replace them responsible first for restoring our rights and taking steps to preserve and protect them.

George Duncan
Peterborough, NH

07.10.07

Faces of failure

Conservatism – and especially neoconservatism – has failed America in the 21st century, as surely as communism failed the Soviet Union in the 20th. Let us count the ways, from one day of reports on Truthout.com:

Alberto Gonzales fires a federal prosecutor because in the absence of a murder weapon, DNA evidence or even a body, he couldn't in good conscience seek the death penalty. Apparently, the Gonzales Justice Dept. lusts after the death penalty -- just as Bush did in Texas.

A new Pew Research poll shows the U.S.' image and reputation has sunk even lower -- right down there with Chavez and Ahmadinejad.

Cheney, after claiming executive privilege to keep all public information in his care private, then claims he's not part of the executive branch – a stance so ludicrous, even he couldn't sustain it. But he had the gall to try it.

"The United States has sunk more than 19 billion dollars into training Iraqi forces, but new army and police units still cannot enforce security, a congressional report warned Wednesday."

Bush continues to issue "signing statements" as he signs bills, which are essentially instructions to federal agencies to ignore the law he is signing.

The inspector general for Iraq reconstruction, Stuart W. Bowen Jr., termed the high level of official corruption in Iraq the "second insurgency," stating that the siphoning-off of U.S. dollars is a major source of funds for the anti-American fighters in the country. It was estimated that last year upward of $100 million in stolen oil funds went directly to the insurgents.

126

Congressman Henry Waxman is trying to track some $22 billion in funds unaccounted for by the KBR division of Halliburton.

Five American soldiers were killed and seven wounded in a coordinated attack in southern Baghdad involving a roadside bomb and rocket-propelled grenades bringing the death toll for the past three months to 329, the deadliest quarter for U.S. troops in Iraq since the war began in March 2003.

And Republicans in the Senate continue to filibuster any Democratic attempt to change anything. In 2008, we must vote Democratic, for the sake of sanity and the future of this country.

George Duncan
Peterborough, NH

07.02.07

Cult of Personality

The Bush administration's interference with numerous scientific and environmental studies has been widely reported as Bush & Co. inject their conservative political venom into every agency of government. Most recent is their attack on the Endangered Species Act as reported in The Christian Science Monitor (7/25). What it illustrates, says the Monitor, is this administration's "resistance to the law." Yes, but much more. What it really shows is the long-standing conservative hostility toward anything that might interfere with the profits of corporate contributors, animals and people included.

We must constantly remember that conservatives do not believe in government. Until recently, the only "government" program conservatives were willing support was the military. Now, under Bush, even that is becoming increasingly privatized. There are as many civilian contractors currently in Iraq as there are troops, and they are growing in both size and influence, even as the uniformed services are being decimated.

Just last week, The Decider announced he would veto a bi-partisan expansion of the State Children's Health Insurance Program, which, for the last ten years has provided healthcare coverage for 6.6 million low-income children whose families do not qualify for Medicaid but cannot afford private insurance on their own. Why? Because he wants to privatize it and drive that money towards his insurance contributors…regardless of the fact that these are families that can't afford insurance.

So what do Republicans do instead of govern since they don't believe in government? They work to limit the rights of people pretty much across the board, they attack any program or institution that depends upon taxes to function, and they use their position to enrich their supporters. Predictably, both Sununu and Gregg voted against the first increase in the minimum wage in ten years.

But perhaps the most telling event of the last few weeks was the testimony of former Surgeon General Richard H. Carmona that the administration's political appointees routinely rewrote his speeches, blocked public health reports for political reasons and screened his travel. Among his charges was that he was required to mention Bush's name three times on each page of any speech he gave. The images that recalls of the so-called cults of personality we've seen like Hitler, Mao, Saddam Hussein, Stalin, <u>Kim Il-sung</u>, Cheney and other dictators is chilling to say the least.

George Duncan
Peterborough, NH

08.01.07

Continuing the Karl Rove tradition

With very little chance of winning the next election honestly, the Republicans are again resorting to the kind of dirty tricks for which they have become justly infamous. Their latest plan would radically change the way California apportions their electoral votes.Rather than awarding all of California's electoral votes to the candidate that wins the popular vote – as does every single state except Maine and Nebraska - their scheme would divvy up California's electoral votes based on the number of congressional districts each candidate wins.

What does this mean? Well, says Senator Barbara Boxer, rather than the Democratic nominee winning all 55 of California's electoral votes in 2008, this new partisan scheme could hand 20 of California's electoral votes to the Republican candidate and only 35 to the Democrat.

"I'm a strong advocate for election reform," says the Senator. "But it's absolutely wrong for California to go it alone. It's just patently unfair for a large 'blue' state like California to change our system for awarding electoral votes while other large states which trend "red" like Texas and Florida don't change their system at the same time. This isn't reform - this is just another partisan power grab by Republican operatives in the Karl Rove tradition."

Meanwhile, back at the White Garrison, The Compassionate Conservative-in-Chief is busy playing another dirty trick on the nation's kids. Failing in the Congress to limit the funds available through the Children's Health Insurance Program, he is now, by presidential fiat free of Congressional oversight, changing the rules under which the funds can be allocated, making it next to impossible for the states to add impoverished children to the coverage. Bush is concerned his insurance industry contributors might lose a few bucks.

And in the dirtiest trick of all, as Bush & Company continues the push to continue the war by manipulating the "surge" findings, keep in mind a recent report in the Christian Science Monitor. According to the nation's top foreign-policy, intelligence, and national-security leaders from across the ideological spectrum, the US is losing the war on terror. In this year's Terrorism Index, released by Foreign Policy magazine, 84 percent of these experts believe the nation is losing the war on terror, while more than 90 percent say the world is growing more dangerous for Americans.

George Duncan
Peterborough, NH

08.30.07

The Baloney Brigade

Now that president Bush has spent a whole four hours in Iraq he's an expert on the surge and he'll be telling us how successful it was over the next several weeks, right after he gets finished writing General Petraeus' report for him. Be prepared for an all-out assault by the White House's baloney brigade singing the praises of the surge. Oh, sure, when 30,000 troops were concentrated in Baghdad, guess what? Violence went down. What a surprise. In fact, last Sunday, Congressman Charles Boustany (R-LA.) claimed that sectarian violence in Baghdad had declined 75 percent! Really? How about the 260 U.S. troop deaths in Iraq during June, July and August, as compiled by the Iraq Coalition Casualty Count (iCasualties.org), the deadliest summer count of the war for U.S. troops.

Mr. Boustany didn't mention those, and neither will Bush. Nor will they mention a NY Times report that deaths across Iraq increased 20 percent since July. Clearly, in John McCain's famous phrase, we're still playing "whack-a-mole" with the insurgents in Iraq. Suppress them over here and they simply pop up over there.

Another reason the overall level of violence in Baghdad is down is that no one can go anywhere safely, so they don't. Between curfews and security restrictions, travel is by armed SUV armada only. Even in the Green Zone, both military and civilians are abandoning the wooden barracks each evening and bedding down in the more secure concrete block administrative buildings.

And the Iraqi police force that's supposed to step up and keep order when our troops stand down is so thoroughly infiltrated by Shiite militia and death squads the entire force needs to be disbanded and rebuilt from scratch. But we won't hear any of this from Bush or Petraeus or Gates in the coming weeks. The baloney brigade will be out in full force as our troops continue to be killed and wounded.

Meanwhile, The Pentagon has drawn up plans for massive airstrikes against 1,200 targets in Iran, designed to annihilate the Iranians' military capability in three days, according to a national security expert. Alexis Debat, director of terrorism and national security at the Nixon Center, said last week that US military planners were not preparing for "pinprick strikes" against Iran's nuclear facilities. "They're about taking out the entire Iranian military," he said.

George Duncan
Peterborough, NH 03458

09.06.07

A nation held captive

I can't recall any similar situation in this country at any time. It seems as though the entire country is being held captive to the wills of two men; Bush and Cheney. It has become cliché now to point out that no one of any consequence supports the Bush agenda in Iraq at this point, save a general or two who's promotions and pensions are sitting on Bush's desk. The Pentagon, Republican leaders and Congress in general, the American people, all of our allies, the troops themselves, and the Iraqis are all opposed, and Cheney's reply is, in effect, "tough darts."

It's been suggested that Bush and Cheney can't leave Iraq until control of the country's oil has been legally turned over to U.S. companies. A measure to that effect is soon to be voted on in the Iraq Parliament.

Others say they just cannot admit defeat. Some even believe Bush may be mentally or emotionally impaired, unable to comprehend reality.

Many of Bush's abuses are just a little too cute to support that view, I think. Like his so-called "signing statements" that have the effect of negating or reversing the intent and enforcement of the bill to which it is attached. Or his current ploy of systematically removing progressive judges from the Federal bench and replacing them with conservative party hacks.

Representative John Conyers, chairman of the House Judiciary Committee, is planning hearings on the signing statements, despite Nancy Pelosi's attempt to mute Democratic responses to the Bush administration's numerous Constitutional abuses.

Indeed, Mr. Conyers is sitting on what may, in the end, be the only way out of this mess, a resolution for impeachment of both Bush and Cheney.

And in response to Ms. Pelosi, many point out that it isn't up to her. That if this is truly a nation of laws, the law should prevail, not Pelosi or anyone else. Impeachment would at least send the message to our allies and rest of the world that we are not what this administration seeks to make us into. That we do not countenance abuses of our Constitution, even by our president. That we do not accept policies of pre-emptive war against anyone we disagree with. And we do not force our system of government upon others at the point of a gun.

George Duncan
Peterborough, NH

1.27.07

Bush Bulls Ahead

It's hard to believe that, with roughly 90 percent of the American people opposed to Bush's so-called "surge" of troops for Iraq, he would so arrogantly add to our difficulties by sending some 30,000 more troops – to do what?

Many top Republicans are also opposed to the plan. The generals on the ground – Casey and Abazaid – are against it – at least they were until Gates went over to do some arm twisting, despite the fact he himself may have reservations. The New York Sun reported last week, "According to two administration officials who asked not to be named, Robert Gates expressed his skepticism about a troop surge in Iraq on his first day on the job, December 18, at a Pentagon meeting with civilians who oversee the Air Force, Army, Navy, and Marines."

The Pentagon is unanimously opposed. Likewise Colin Powell. Even President Ford came out against the pre-emption policy posthumously, thanks to Bob Woodward. And finally, the troops are opposed. Military Times reports, " The American military - once a staunch supporter of President Bush and the Iraq war - has grown increasingly pessimistic about chances for victory, according to the 2006 Military Times Poll. For the first time, more troops disapprove of the president's handling of the war than approve of it. Barely one-third of service members approve of the way the president is handling the war. Only 35 percent of the military members polled this year said they approve of the way President Bush is handling the war, while 42 percent said they disapproved. The president's approval rating among the military is only slightly higher than for the population as a whole."

The L.A. Times points to key opposition from Democrats, especially Joe Biden: "Sen. Joseph R. Biden Jr. (D-Del.), the incoming chairman of the

Foreign Relations Committee, said Tuesday that he intended to call key administration officials, including Secretary of State Condoleezza Rice, to testify at as many as a dozen hearings. At the same time, the chairmen of both chambers' armed services committees and of the House International Relations Committee also plan to hold hearings President Harry Truman, who knew something about committing troops, said, "There is nothing more foolish than to think that war can be stopped by war. You don't prevent anything but peace."

George Duncan
Peterborough, NH

1.01.07

Bush's Kabuki Surge

As we salute General Petraeus' dedication to duty and years of distinguished service to his country, we must also recognize that it is precisely that sterling reputation that the Bush administration is so cynically attempting to use against the honest questioners in the Congress, the press and the American people -- much as they used Colin Powell's reputation for straight shooting when they sent him to the U.N. to lie for them.

The mountain of evidence challenging or refuting the general's findings that has emerged from so many non-partisan sources makes his appearance before the Congress just another act in the Bush administration's continuing Kabuki theater attempt to disguise his bankrupt policies in Iraq.

Amazing that at no time did anyone mention, for example, that one reason Sunni leaders have signed on to oppose al Qaeda in al Anbar is WE'RE PAYING THEM! And arming them so they can protect themselves from the Shiites. Another reason, as one Iraqi stated, is they got tired of being told by al Qaeda operatives who they could marry and what mosque to attend. The ones who weren't murdered by Shiite death squads, that is. Furthermore, there simply aren't that many Sunnis left around Baghdad, as the Shiites systematically evict them from their homes at gunpoint and resell the houses to Shiites. No real estate slump there! Petraeus and Crocker actually tried to spin that as a positive. The Sunnis were leaving to "seek safety" they said. Yikes!

Petraeus displayed a chart supposedly showing civilian casualties down for five weeks. He ignored the fact that the chart actually showed an increase for one of those weeks. Another chart showed that "ethno-sectarian" deaths --- that's Bushspeak for civil war, since he dare not speak that truth -- were down in August from July, but still higher than in June.

The final insult came when Senator John Warner asked Petraeus point blank: "Does the [Iraq war] make America safer?" Petraeus replied, "I don't know, actually. I have not sat down and sorted in my own mind." He advocates pursuing Bush's course of action in Iraq but he cannot attest that the effort is crucial for America's safety? I'm sure the troops in Iraq will be delighted to learn that their commander has no more idea why they're there than the rest of us.

George Duncan
Peterborough, NH

01.27.07

Cronies and Phonies

The Bush Justice Department, which may be an oxymoron, has been engaged in what can only be described as a political purge of our federal prosecutors as The Washington Post announced last week, "An eighth U.S. attorney announced her resignation yesterday, the latest in a wave of forced departures of federal prosecutors who have clashed with the Justice Department over the death penalty and other issues." Seven others, six of which had excellent performance reviews, have been forced to resign since early December.

Creating openings through resignations allows the Attorney General to appoint replacements under a clause in the Patriot Act, thus bypassing the Senate confirmation process. Democrats in the Senate see this as yet another instance of Bush's rampant cronyism and an effort to punish any prosecutor who's work might negatively affect a Republican ally. Needless to say, the replacements all pass the various conservative litmus tests.

Dianne Feinstein has sponsored a bill that would help to plug the hole Bush is trying to drive his sycophants through and it should be noted that three prominent Republicans, Arlen Specter, Charles Grassley and Orrin Hatch, have signed on. But the larger issue is this administration's blatant attempt to hijack your government and mine. No one quarrels with a president's right to fill vacancies with qualified party people if approved by the Senate. But creating the vacancies by firing perfectly competent, experienced people in order to bypass Senate scrutiny is another matter.

We've already seen how Bush had at least a half dozen regulatory agency heads forced out and replaced by cronies. Now, through executive order, he's extending that to additional federal agencies that enforce health, safety and environmental protections. What's more, these agencies must now submit their work for approval by these political hacks, and, when necessary, the president himself, effectively creating a politically driven form of censorship. The last time I heard of anything similar was the operation of the various soviets and worker's organizations in Lenin's Soviet Union.

As the 2008 Senate campaigns get under way, we must ask our state's two senators in what ways they helped or hindered these various arrogations of presidential power in violation of existing law. Existing, that is, before Bush and company rewrote or circumvented them to suit their purpose.

George Duncan
Peterborough, NH

01.01.07

Even the troops are opposed

Even the troops are opposed. Military Times reports, " The American military - once a staunch supporter of President Bush and the Iraq war - has grown increasingly pessimistic about chances for victory, according to the 2006 Military Times Poll. For the first time, more troops disapprove of the president's handling of the war than approve of it. Barely one-third of service members approve of the way the president is handling the war. Only 35 percent of the military members polled this year said they approve of the way President Bush is handling the war, while 42 percent said they disapproved. The president's approval rating among the military is only slightly higher than for the population as a whole."

George Duncan
Peterborough, NH

1.07.07

Oil, Oil, Oil

It looks like the Bush Administration may have finally achieved, after 4 years of war and tens of thousands of American and Iraqi deaths, what it set out to accomplish with the illegal invasion of Iraq in 2003. President Bush is quietly negotiating an agreement with Iraqi Prime Minister Nouri al-Maliki to keep our troops there indefinitely--**an agreement that could include permanent bases and a massive military presence for years!** Bush is trying to tie the hands of the next administration to keep us in Iraq for the foreseeable future. a deal with the so-called Iraqi government to protect the Iraq oil fields with a permanent commitment of American troops and lives, and to guarantee access to the oil for U.S. companies. No doubt daddy and his Carlyle partners are proud.

This is a pivotal moment—the agreement is still in the planning stages and if we don't act now, we could be stuck in Iraq for decades.

Congress can stop the president from setting up permanent bases in Iraq and block an indefinite occupation—but it's not clear that they will. They need to feel a groundswell of pressure from voters immediately and loudly so they act on this quickly.

George Duncan
Peterborough, NH

09.11.07

Socialized Medicine

Conservative lawmakers in the House of Representatives sided with President Bush yesterday in denying millions of children the opportunity to receive health insurance. Congress fell 13 votes short of the two-thirds majority needed to override Bush's veto of the popular and successful State Children's Health Insurance Program (SCHIP), but in doing so, picked up eight votes from the original House vote just a few weeks ago. Forty-four Republicans voted for the override. White House spokeswoman Dana Perino triumphantly declared, "We won this round on SCHIP." For the White House, indeed the debate about expanding SCHIP was a political game to be won or lost. But for millions of children who were denied health care coverage because of Bush's veto, yesterday's vote was a somber reminder that the president stands squarely against their interests.

Eight in 10 Americans favor expanding the State Children's Health Insurance Program," and only 22 percent approve of Bush's handling of the issue. Congressional leaders "vow[ed] to keep up the fight," and pledged to re-ignite the legislation in the very near future. For the cost of just 41 days of war in Iraq, the nation could insure 10 million children for one year.

George Duncan
Peterborough, NH

10.19.07

The Bush Crucible

I had the pleasure of attending The Small Pond Productions' presentation of Arthur Miller's "The Crucible" last week. A dramatization of the Salem witch trials, it is generally considered a commentary on the McCarthy hearings of the Fifties – another conservative triumph – in which an authoritarian regime arrogantly assumes God-given dictatorial powers to persecute a gaggle of young girls guilty little more than group hysteria. While the echoes of McCarthyism ring loud and clear, I was struck by the many similarities to today's authoritarianism and the Bush administration's war on terrorism.

Energizing the events in Salem was the same twisting of logic and corruption of common sense in the service of supporting foregone conclusions and opinion that we have seen from Bush and company these last four years. There was the immediate condemnation of the few – however reputable – who spoke out against the Puritan clergy's prosecution of the girls. At one point the inquisitor even says, "You must be with the court or against it." There was the same denial of legal counsel as we have seen in Guantanamo and elsewhere. "The Crucible" also makes a compelling argument against the current tendencies among Republicans to meld religion with government in violation of the Constitution's opening sentence (First Amendment).

The lesson here, I think, is that authoritarianism can take on a life of its own. John Dean (of Watergate fame) has brought the subject starkly up to date in his recent book, "Conservatives Without Conscience" which I recommend to anyone concerned with where our country is headed.

I wish I could feel confident that simply electing a Democratic president would solve it, but as a recent Newsweek article warns, Bush/Cheney's "unitary executive" concept and the dictatorial powers it assumes has survived intact and will pass on unchallenged to the next president, whomever he or she may be. When Barack Obama came to Peterborough I was asked if I had any questions I would like to ask him. My question was what he thought about the unitary executive concept and what, if anything would he do about it if elected. Turned out he didn't take questions, but I think it's something we should find out about all the candidates of both parties.

George Duncan
Peterborough, NH

01.07.07

The Republicans' War

It's pure nonsense to blame the Democratic majority in Congress for failing to get us out of Iraq as promised. Their majority is simply too slim to overcome Republican filibusters or a Bush veto. Slate reports, "Senate Republicans blocked a measure that was thought to be the best chance lawmakers had to alter Iraq policy. Sen. Jim Webb's proposal would have mandated that active-duty troops couldn't be redeployed to Iraq or Afghanistan unless they were given as much time at home as they had spent in the war zone. Webb, a Democrat from Virginia, had a prominent GOP co-sponsor in Sen. Chuck Hagel but the proposal gathered support from only six Republicans, so it fell four votes short of the 60 necessary to prevent a filibuster. It now seems clear Democrats won't be able to get Republicans to support any measure that would affect troop levels in Iraq."

So long as Republicans in Congress continue to blindly support George Bush and their party's "base" rather than respond to the clear desires of the American people as they have sworn to do, our troops will continue to be killed in the service of the Bush/Cheney debacle, Iraqis will continue to die from a variety of causes and the nation will continue to be drawn further into war. How any rational being can be fooled by Bush's shell game with the 30,000 troop surge is beyond me. And now Bush is asking for another $200 billion making 2008 the most costly year yet. A discussion aired on C-Span this weekend by leading journalists and retired military sponsored by the Kennedy School of Government at Harvard exposed much of the bushwa surrounding so-called progress in Anbar and the effects of the surge in Baghdad.

So if you know any Republicans who might care more about the troops and about the daily carnage in Iraq than they do the president (other than Gregg or Sununu, sad to say), and if you'd like to see this obscene war wound down, ask them to support the Democrats in Congress because despite numerous attempts, they can't do it without Republican votes. In this matter, at least, it's the Republicans who are "controlling" Congress, not the Democrats, and they are setting the stage for unlimited involvement of our troops in Iraq. Clearly, after these last votes, Iraq is the Republicans' war.

George Duncan
Peterborough, NH

01.07.07

There he goes again

So apparently, we're all just too stupid to understand what the Great Decider has decided. That must apply to the foreign ministers of all of our allies as well, including Great Britain which has just announced significant troop reductions co-incident with the "surge." On 60 Minutes, Bush said part of his job is to be "Educator in Chief" which amounts to appearing before hand-picked and/or military audiences and endlessly repeating the same 3-4 talking points until we're all ready to scream.

And if you saw Tony Snow's pathetic tap dance around Chris Matthews' direct questions about a possible invasion of Iran, you'd know that's absolutely next on the agenda.

Bush's complaint on 60 Minutes was that opponents of the so-called strategy were "condemning it before they've tried it." Huh? In this case, "trying" it is the same as doing it. As Yoda says, there is no try. This isn't a jacket you slip on and if it doesn't fit, slip it off. Once our troops are engaged in the streets of Baghdad, there will be no turning back. And Gates says we'll probably know the results in 4 to 6 months. Six months! And then begin a withdrawal?

If past performance is any guide, we'll probably see those Iraqi forces fold in a lot less than six months. It'll be more like six days -- assuming they show up at all -- and there our guys will be, exposed like fish in a barrel. No air support, no artillery. Even tanks will find it tough going in those city streets.

In his speech on the "New Way Forward," Bush appeared to make a case for continued war in Iraq but Mark Seibel of the McClatchy Newspapers points out a number of inaccuracies in the president's selective account of events and dates, clearly calculated to deflect blame from policy foulups and place it on the "insurgents." They're too detailed to recount here, but it's clear Bush is at it again – cooking the books to make his case.

"Madam Secretary," Senator Bill Nelson, (D-Fla.) said to Condi Rice, "I have supported you and the administration on the war, and I cannot continue to support the administration's position. I have not been told the truth over and over again by administration witnesses, and the American people have not been told the truth." And we still haven't.

George Duncan
Peterborough NH

10.21.07

Where White is Black

With regard to the new National Intelligence Estimate, the Inter-Press Agency reported back in early November, "An NIE on Iran has been held up for more than a year in an effort to force the intelligence community to remove dissenting judgments on the Iranian nuclear program, and thus make the document more supportive of U.S. Vice President Dick Cheney's militarily aggressive policy toward Iran, according to accounts of the process provided by two former Central Intelligence Agency officers. "The White House wants a document that it can use as evidence for its Iran policy," said former CIA officer Philip Giraldi.

A year! Not months as we've been told. Now the findings are public and we see the ease with which President Bush deliberately misrepresents the facts to the American people purely to advance his agenda, even to threatening "World War III" to scare people into sticking with Republicans in November. Then, of course, the conservative slime machine attacks the report as though sixteen agencies, each with dozens of analysts, could secretly conspire to produce an anti-administration finding.

Pity he can't simply stand up like the man he pretends to be and say, "Fortunately, recent intelligence findings show that earlier estimates of Iran's nuclear capabilities were unfounded. As a result, we can now pursue diplomatic solutions to the Iran threat which, although greatly diminished, still exists over the longer term."

MoveOn's Ilyse Hogue writes: "This morning, (President Bush) held a news conference where he actually tried to portray the news that Iran isn't building a bomb as yet another reason to confront Iran! He also said he hadn't known about the new evidence—a fact contradicted by his own

151

National Security Adviser. It's Iraq all over again. Bush is willing to ignore intelligence and lie to move us towards another war."

What I want to know is (1) how bald do the lies have to get before the press calls spade a spade, and (2) why does the Washington Press Corps continue to meet in the White House? Do they really believe that this man has anything of value left to smirk?...say?

George Duncan
Peterborough, NH 03458

12.04.07

Bush's Anti-Healthcare Budget

After raising the debt ceiling four times in five years, after trying to suck $600 billion out of the system over the next five years -- $1.9 trillion over the next ten – through tax cuts for the wealthy, after adding $100 billion in debt for his misbegotten war in Iraq (on top of $70 billion already allocated), George Bush has suddenly discovered the budget deficit. Now that Democrats control the Congress, Bush wants to balance the budget. And guess where he intends to balance it; on the backs of the poor and elderly through $77 billion in cuts in Medicare and Medicaid.

While the President would spend $60 billion to fatten the wallets of military contractors, he wants to cut payments to health-care providers and force elder citizens to pay more for physician services and prescription drug coverage. He also wants to cut health insurance for children in working class families. Point these facts out to Republicans and you're accused of waging class warfare – when it's the Republicans who have been gunning for Medicare, Medicaid and Social Security since the day those programs were passed.

By 2025, the over 65 cohort of New Hampshire citizens will have increased by 97%. That means a greater reliance by New Hampshirites on Social Security, Medicare and Medicaid than ever before in our history. If that group includes you or your parents, you'll want to keep our state and federal legislators' feet to the fire in saving and strengthening those program, not gutting them. Write and call our representatives and tell them where you stand.

George Duncan
Peterborough, NH

2.11.07

Capitalism

Republicans are fond of saying they favor smaller government. The rest of us assume that's because smaller government means lower taxes and who can argue with paying less taxes, right? Wrong. Lower taxes may be a by-product of smaller government, and no doubt many Republicans take it just that far and no further. But the Republicans in power: the Roves, the Cheneys, the Wolfowitz's, the Bush's and all the other the American Enterprise Institute Neocons know better. Truth is, they're afraid of big government – government that might actually "promote the general welfare" – because promoting the general welfare – providing healthcare and education, protecting the environment, establishing economic safety nets, helping the disadvantaged and more – costs money. And that means taxes with their fair share increasing proportionately.

More importantly, however, is how promoting the general welfare conflicts with the free market economy they lust after. "Free" in this instance means freedom from fair labor practices, a living wage and the right to unionize. Freedom from safe workplaces and employer-supported healthcare. Freedom from clean air and water rules for industry and so on.

We're seeing every day how free market policies like NAFTA and CAFTA are sending America's high paying jobs overseas to third world countries where the salaries are lower, and the workplace restrictions non-existent and how they're being replaced here with lower paying, no-benefit (no union!) service jobs. There may be more of them as free marketeers love to point out. There better be, because many families need two or three of them to survive. But these jobs are lowering the American standard of living, not raising it.

We've also seen, most recently, how the profit motive, which drives the free market economy, can backfire. Ask anyone who was sold a no-money-down-no-payments-for-five-years mortgage that's now tanking, and see what that whole money grab is doing to our 401K's.

Americans have long since accepted the idea of two working parents in every household (we're modern!) along with daycare, "latchkey" kids, etc. (how's that for raising the standard of living?), so to really see the effects of free markets you have to look at cultures where the wives don't work outside the home. Like Chile. That's where, as Naomi Klein points out in her amazing book, "Shock Doctrine," Milton Friedman sent his free market economists to spread the capitalist doctrine. The people's response was to democratically elect a Socialist, Salvador Allende, in the hope he would provide some measure of social and economic protection. Hey, can't have that in our hemisphere, who do they think they are? So to promote democratic capitalism in Chile whether the people wanted it or not (sound familiar?), the CIA assassinated Allende and replaced him with the fascist, Pinochet. Take that, you liberal wussies!

George Duncan
Peterborough, NH

10.21.07

Fast and Loose

President Bush has signed a directive that gives the White House much greater control over the rules and policy statements that the government develops to protect public health, safety, the environment, civil rights and privacy. In an executive order published last week in the Federal Register, Mr. Bush said that each agency must have a regulatory policy office run by a political appointee, to supervise the development of rules and documents providing guidance to regulated industries. The White House will thus have a gatekeeper in each agency to analyze the costs and the benefits of new rules and to make sure the agencies carry out the president's priorities Besides placing political appointees in charge of rule making, Mr. Bush said agencies must give the White House an opportunity to review "any significant guidance documents" before they are issued.

* * *

The administration is replacing U.S. Attorneys throughout the country. How'd they get that power?

It was an obscure provision in the USA PATRIOT Improvement and Reauthorization Act, and it didn't take them very long to use it. The president signed it into law in March of last year -- by June, they were already moving to replace unwanted prosecutors. Former Arkansas USA Bud Cummins told the Wall Street Journal that "a top Justice official asked for his resignation in June, saying the White House wanted to give another person the opportunity to serve." Cummins was finally forced out in December, replaced with Timothy Griffin, formerly the research director of the Republican National Committee.

As a way of thwarting global warming discussions, Bush had his operatives go through scientific studies and reports and delete the phrases "global warming" and "climate change." He has also forbidden members of his administration from using the terms in conversation. How's that for freedom of speech?

George Duncan
Peterborough, NH

1.30.07

Rethinking the "S" Word

When the House failed to override Bush's veto of the SCHIP program, thanks mostly to Republican intransigence, Bush spokeswoman Dana Perino triumphantly declared, "We won this round on SCHIP." Said The Center for American Progress, "For the White House, indeed, the debate about expanding SCHIP was a political game to be won or lost. But for millions of children who were denied health care coverage because of Bush's veto, yesterday's vote was a somber reminder that the president stands squarely against their interests."

"Make no mistake about it," said Rep. Jeb Hensarling, (R-Texas), the chairman of the conservative Republican Study Committee. "This bill is a government-run, socialized medicine wolf masquerading in the sheepskin of children's health care."

The Oxford American Dictionary defines socialized medicine as "The provision of medical and hospital care for all by means of public funds." What a concept! Use the public's money to guarantee medical and hospital care for the public! Key phrase, "for all." How about your own insurance, Jeb? Clearly, you and the rest of Congress don't mind using public money – socialized medicine – to insure yourselves and your families. And Republicans don't mind spending $680 billion in a disastrous invasion and occupation of Iraq. How does the public feel about that?

The Center of American Progress reports: "Eight in 10 Americans favor expanding the State Children's Health Insurance Program, and only 22 percent approve of Bush's handling of the issue. For the cost of just 41 days of war in Iraq, the nation could insure 10 million children for one year."

But as Paul Krugman pointed out, "The worst thing from Bush's point of view, is a government program that actually does help people. So the SCHIP is a really bad thing, because it works so well. It might lead people to say, well, if we can do this for children, why can't we do it for lots of other people who need guaranteed health care? So it's the determination, on his part, to do this veto, even though there's a short-term political cost, because they're deathly afraid that people will look at SCHIP and say, gee, actually the government can do some good."

George Duncan
Peterborough, NH

11.10.07

The Don Quixote Candidate

Barack Obama is an honorable man, no doubt. His heart is pure and he wants only the best for America. But when he touts his ideas for "a new kind of politics" and summons us to "turn the page," I'm afraid he's beating, not so much a dead horse, as one that's not quite ready to run.

As a Washington Post article points out, Democrats are angry. For seven years now, we've watched the trashing of our government and the constitution in a manner that we thought could only happen in fiction. Every week we watch the mounting casualty figures from Iraq, witness the agonies of the families and see our young men and women get killed and maimed purely to feed one man's seemingly limitless lust for power. We've uncovered lie after lie about that war with more unearthed almost weekly. We've seen the most cynical manipulation of the institutions of democracy with no accountability from anyone. And we've seen people we thought better of – from supposedly responsible legislators to friends and associates – support and protect the entire process with pig-headed insistence that flies in the face of all evidence to the contrary. Simply watching the recent broadcast of "Frontline" as it detailed the arrogant march to power that the Bush administration and their legal sycophants have foisted upon the American public is enough to ache for impeachment.

Anyone who speaks out gets slimed – the typical Cheney-Rove-Bush response – as unpatriotic and worse. And like Howard Beale, many Democrats are "mad as hell and not going to take it anymore."

I'm sure at least some of Hillary's lead in the polls is because she has the street smarts to deal with any sensible Republicans that may be left and actually effect change. If we can reclaim our government and restore our sanity with a hiatus of at least four years of progressive leadership, maybe we'll be willing to talk. If we can wind down the war, the horrors of that stupidity might press less painfully on our consciousness. Like a latter day Don Quixote, Barack clearly commands the moral high ground in this election. But with our democracy in peril and our troops in harm's way, this may not be the time for tilting at windmills.

George Duncan
Peterborough, NH

10.22.07

The War President

The Bush-Petraeus report reminds me of the time the Bush administration planted an article on a shipment of aluminum tubes to Iraq -- supposedly for a nuclear reactor -- in the New York Times via their lackey, Judith Miller and then had their heavy hitters go on Sunday talk shows and point to the article with "An article in today's New York Times says..." In similar fashion, Bush flew to Iraq to make sure Petraeus knows what he wants in the findings, then points to Petraeus' report as vindication of his policy.

About a week ago, Bush was addressing the VFW: "I stand before you as a war time president," he proudly proclaimed.. And I had to think, isn't that what this has been about from day one? That Bush/Rove/Cheney saw war as a sure way to secure the president's reelection and the Republican party's majority in Congress. And there was Bush, the Vietnam draft dodger and failed Air National Guard pilot, standing before men who have served suggesting that he's one of them -- because he's a "war time president?" Yuck!

George Duncan
Peterborough, NH

9.12.07

162

In politics as in life, love trumps hate

Recently, George Lakoff, (Rockridgeinstitute.org), offered a reply to the conservative contention that liberals "hate America." It's an accusation so mindless and repugnant (yet one I experienced myself from someone I thought knew better), that I had to consider my own reply: No. Liberals love America's democracy and want to return it to the nation. What we hate is the "ends justifies the means" philosophy with which you have attempted to destroy 230 years of constitutional democracy with phony "findings" and arrogant assertions of power, unsubstantiated by any recognized authority.

Liberals love America's freedom from unreasonable search and seizure as guaranteed in the 4th amendment to the Constitution. What we hate is secretly tapping phones and seizing citizens' financial records without judicial review. We love America's transparency of government and the accessibility of its workings to the people as assured by the Freedom of Information Act among others. What we hate is the secrecy you hide behind with your equally transparent claims of security and executive privilege.

We love America's freedom of speech and expression. What we hate is the way you trash and slime anyone with an opposing view. We love thoughtful dialog to determine the best governance for the greatest good. What we hate is the simplistic, bumper-sticker solutions you bring to complex issues. You rant and rave against "government spending," for example, while avoiding any mention of what the "spending" might provide, like better access to healthcare for millions of uninsured kids.

Liberals recognize that only the power and resources of a collective government can effectively meet people's needs and assure social justice in today's increasingly complex society while you oppose government, period. For you, government means services for people – to "promote the general welfare" – and even for a constitutional originalist, that costs money, which means taxes, which means you may be asked to contribute your fair share!

We love that in America we are all free to believe in whatever God we choose – or no God at all if we choose – but we hate it when you bring your personal religious beliefs into the public square and try to force them on others. In an early recognition of the wisdom of separation of church and state, Jesus said, "Render unto Caesar the things that are Caesar's and unto God the things that are God's." Let's keep it that way.

George Duncan
Peterborough, NH

11.28.07

2008

The Iraq Industry

When Barack Obama outpulls Hillary in a primary 64 to 34 percent, it's called a "blowout." But when those same numbers are applied to the number of Americans who oppose the Iraq war – 64 percent against, 34 percent in favor according to CNN – it's ignored by everyone from the corporate media to the Republicans in Congress. Those numbers are after the so-called "surge." Pretty much the same as they were before the surge.

And what a PR stunt that's been. Flood a street corner with cops and the crime rate goes down. Big whoop. But the real reason the violence has diminished has to do with the machinations of the Shiites and Sunnis among themselves and Moqtada al Sadr declaring a six-month cease fire with his Mahdi Army while he played politics. That ends this month.

I've been struck in recent months by the disparities in reportage between the so-called mainstream (or corporate media, as some would have it) and numerous first person articles published in such magazines as The New Yorker, Esquire, Vanity Fair and others, frequently by military personnel still in or recently returned from the field. It's like reading about two different wars. Most painful was the thrust of one piece showing that the increase in PTSD among our returning troops is not from the rigors of combat, for which they are trained and ready, but from the effects of killing civilians, for which they are not.

Recently Harold Bloom, Yale professor of literature and cultural critic, compared our involvement in Iraq with the fall of Rome. "The war is what Parthia was to Rome," he said, referring to the Persian empire that bogged the Empire down in three centuries of war. "Imagine, he said, "the complete madness in trying to occupy a large Arab country in the middle of the Arab world, a culture we know precious little about, and who speaks a language only a handful of our specialists can speak, with armed forces who we have limited control of and with a large army of private soldiers…the whole thing is scandal…a series of lies." (935 lies according to the Centre for Public Integrity). Then he added, I don't understand the motivation for the war, but I suspect the real reason for the war … is that it simply is a profitable machine." To which Halliburton and The Carlyle Group chant "Amen."

George Duncan
Peterborough, NH

02.13.08

How liberal are you?

Frank Rich wrote in a recent Times column: "We keep hearing that America is "a center-right nation" — apparently because the percentages of Americans who call themselves conservative (34), moderate (44) and liberal (22) remain virtually unchanged from four years ago. But if we've learned anything this year, surely it's that labels are overrated.

Those same polls find that more and more self-described conservatives no longer consider themselves Republicans. Americans now say they favor government doing more (51 percent), not less (43) — an 11-point swing since 2004 — and they still overwhelmingly reject the Iraq war. That's a centrist country tilting center-left, and that's the majority who voted for Obama."

David Sirota says on Salon, "When George W. Bush wins by 3 million votes, the braindead megaphone blares announcements about a conservative mandate that Democrats must respect. When Obama wins by twice as much, the same megaphone roars about Democrats having no mandate to do anything other than appease conservatives." Really? According to post-election polls, says Sirota, 70 percent of Americans say they want conservatives to help this progressive president enact his decidedly progressive agenda.

Where do you stand on the liberal-conservative continuum? Following are the various definitions and entries for the word "liberal" as found in dictionary.com, clearly, a non-partisan source. If you consider yourself Republican or conservative, which of these do not apply to you?

1. Favorable to or in accord with concepts of maximum individual freedom possible, esp. as guaranteed by law and secured by governmental protection of civil liberties.
2. Favoring or permitting freedom of action, esp. with respect to matters of personal belief or expression.
3. of or pertaining to representational forms of government rather than aristocracies and monarchies.
4. free from prejudice or bigotry; tolerant.

As for that favorite Republican whipping boy, *The New York Times* and it's so-called liberal bias, executive editor Bill Keller agrees, but he may define liberal a bit differently: "in the sense that a liberal arts college is liberal – generally secular in outlook, disinclined to take things on faith, nondogmatic, tolerant and curious about a wide range of views and behaviors." You too? What a surprise!

George Duncan
Peterborough, NH

11.08.08

Can He Lead?

Senator McCain has taken to making his campaign primarily about Barack Obama – presumably so we'll look less closely at McCain. His main tactic is to cast doubt on Obama's ability with the rhetorical trick of asking a loaded question repetitively until people who may not be paying close attention will take it as some sort of statement. The question, however, "Can he lead?" is easily answered firmly in the positive by looking no further than the current gasoline price crisis.

Where McCain's solution is the same old tired conservative mantra; drill drill drill, (greased by more than $2 million in oil company "contributions"), Mr. Obama is bringing true leadership to the issue, pointing out the falseness of the drilling promise as attested by the U.S. Department of Energy's Energy Information Administration (EIA). That's called LEADERSHIP, especially when the drilling idea has found favor, however flawed, with the people.

Put McCain's drilling policy together with Bush's observation that we're addicted to oil and you have the equivalent of taking away an alcoholic's trusty pint and handing him a half gallon. Of course bringing down the price of oil by adding more oil, pretending that's possible, renders research and development of many of the alternative energy sources less financially attractive. During the 70's oil embargo, I recall a Saudi prince saying about the energy alternatives that were being touted at the time that as soon as they showed any promise, all OPEC had to do was lower the price and those ideas went away. So maybe we should keep the price at the pump high enough to encourage investment in solar, wind, biomass and other technologies. McCain wants 45 nuclear reactors. Funded how? And if nuclear is such a great way to go, how come no one's invested a nickel in it in twenty years? Can you spell Chernobyl?

But McCain really doesn't care about any of this. He's content to spin out one lie and distortion after another so he doesn't have to discuss his policies on Social Security (a "disaster," give it to Wall Street); healthcare (tax employers), taxes (extend Bush's giveaways to the wealthy), oil profits (give them billions in tax breaks), women's reproductive rights (appoint judges to end them) -- and then there's the Bush/McCain/Iraq occupation/Iran war. Ready for Bush II?

George Duncan
Peterborough, NH

8.11.08

Grand Delusions

Juan Cole, Distinguished University Professor of History at the University of Michigan and nationally recognized Middle East scholar wrote of the surge, "Each year of George W. Bush's war in Iraq has been represented by a thematic falsehood. That Iraq is now calm or more stable is only the latest in a series of such whoppers, which the mainstream press eagerly repeats. Sen. John McCain, in turn, has now taken to dangling the bait of 'total victory' before the American public, and some opinion polls suggest that Americans are swallowing it, hook, line and sinker." (http://www.salon.com/ opinion/ feature/2008 / 03/19/iraq_five.htm).

We can only hope that more information will be revealed soon rather than the long delays that have been the case thus far to pierce the delusions Bush and McCain are foisting upon the people. For a military man, McCain seems extraordinarily cavalier about the 4,000 US military deaths, and appears incapable of offering any description of what would constitute "victory." I'd like to ask him why "regime change" with a democratically elected parliament, a new constitution and a democratically elected Prime Minister doesn't meet the test of victory as described by the administration back in 2003?

But the economics of the war is where McCain's delusions really get weird. Nobel Laureate economist Joseph Stiglitz puts the cost of the war at $3 trillion, while adding some $2.5 trillion to the national debt. For a fraction of which, Stiglitz says, "we could have put Social Security on a sound footing for the next half-century or more." McCain not only wants to continue the war regardless of length or cost, his solution to the Social Security issue is to exhume Bush's privatizing fantasy. One day's cost of this war could make a year of college affordable for 160,000 low-income students, for just one example. Rather than reduce nonessential spending programs as with past wars, McCain would extend the Bush tax cuts.

Patriotism to me, extends beyond the battlefield. It encompasses the well being of the people, the military and the economy. And when it comes to other nations, it doesn't impose democracy upon a people who never asked for it, are not prepared for it, and who clearly prefer the theocracy they have known for centuries. Democracy grows though attraction, not promotion.

George Duncan
Peterborough, NH

4.13.08

Let's lose the labels and seek 21st century solutions

A Republican colleague of mine once declared that "a conservative is a person with something to conserve." "Yes," I replied, "at everyone else's expense." Imagine my surprise earlier this month when Times columnist Frank Rich opined, "The whole point of the Bush-Rove way of doing business is that principles, coherent governance and even ideology must always be sacrificed for political expediency, no matter the cost to the public good."

There could be no group of conservatives more strongly opposed to "socialism" than the mandarins of Wall Street and Washington who crafted the bailout plan for the country's banks as the market melted down. Yet, they did so with both presidential candidates signing off on it, because, repugnant as it may have been to most of them, it was what they could do halt the slide.

It's a relevant point, for as President Obama moves forward to rebuild confidence in the markets and set the stage for job growth, he's going need everyone's support in crafting solutions and he'll have a tougher time doing that if we allow ourselves to be tied down by labels.

Frank Zeidler, an American socialist who served as the mayor of Milwaukee from 1948 to 1960 said, "Socialism as we attempted to practice it here believes that people working together for a common good can produce a greater benefit both for society and for the individual than can a society in which everyone is shrewdly seeking their own self-interest."

Updating Zeidler, historian Sean Wilentz writes in a recent Newsweek, "Amid what Republicans and Democrats agree is the worst financial catastrophe since the Great Depression, government has become the solution again – the only conceivable one – and it seems that it will remain so for a long time to come."

John McCain was a 20th century warrior caught in a 21st century battle. The message of this election is that the policies that have brought us to these circumstances will not solve them, at home or abroad. It's time for thoughtful Republicans to join Democrats in finding new solutions that work for the common good and dump the stupid labels on the trash heap of history where they belong. Who knows but that in that effort, they might even discover they have the makings of a relevant and resurgent Republican party.

George Duncan
Peterborough, NH

11.08.08

Sorry, Bill

Knowing that roughly half the folks who read my letters will disagree with them, I decided some time back not to respond to the (so far surprisingly few) push back letters that might appear in these pages. However, I must admit that Bill Taylor's recent missive makes a point. My choice of prose in an earlier post was overly purple, driven, no doubt, by my distaste for the calumny and slander of the Republican swift boaters and their ilk. Let's hear it for their ilk. (Isn't it amazing how Barack Obama has successfully hidden his Muslim terrorist identity all these years behind a facade of community organizer, social activist, state senator, U.S. Senator and nice guy candidate? Must be a sleeper agent.) Also, I admit to an irresistible impulse to hit "send." So, sorry, Bill. If you'll drag your knuckles over to say hello when you see me around, I'll apologize in person.

That said, it has seemed odd to me how few responses to Bushevik criticisms have appeared in the last 7 years. Where is Vic Mangini when we need him?

Especially with the heckofajob Bush has done these last 7 years! Let's see, there's the Iraq war that, as our intrepid "War President," he lied us into to the tune of 4,000+ American dead, tens of thousands severely wounded, $535 billion in treasure gone and counting (that's $341.4 million per day)... Well, maybe not.

How about the econ -- Ooops. Are you better off now than you were an hour ago? How do you like free markets so far?

Then there was his All Funding Left Behind program for the school kids; trying to dump Social Security into that dark stock market night; sending more than 1 million Gulf Coast folks inland for an extended vacation;

remembering his good wealthy friends with hefty tax cuts – that the rest of us will have to pay for; vetoing healthcare for kids (class act, that); illegally torturing prisoners; illegally tapping his constituents' phones (at least 30 felonies there); thumbing his nose at the Constitution (maybe someone will read it to him some day); and on and on.

So, sorry again, Bill, I just get p.o.'d when the folks who supported and facilitated and praised all that have the gall to slime innocent people. I'm sure it's just me.

George Duncan
Peterborough, NH

08.11.08

Fact-Checking McCain's Tax Lies

The McCain campaign just released another ad accusing Barack Obama of planning to raise taxes on working families earning over $42,000 which Fact Checker says is "simply false."

FactCheck.org is the home of the FactChecker, a non-partisan initiative of the University of Pennsylvania's Annenberg Public Policy Center. In examining John McCain's statements about Barack Obama's tax policies, they determined the following:

"A radio ad claims the measure Obama supported would have raised taxes on "families" making $42,000, which is simply false. Even a single mother with one child would have been able to make $58,650 without being affected. A family of four with income up to $90,000 would not have been affected."

Checking further, FactChecker found a TV ad that claims in a graphic that Obama would 'raise taxes on middle class.' In fact, Obama's plan promises cuts for middle-income taxpayers and would increase rates only for persons with family incomes above $250,000 or with individual incomes above $200,000.

Another ad claims Obama would increase taxes "on the sale of your home." "In fact," says FactChecker, "home-sale profits of up to $500,000 per couple would continue to be exempt from capital gains taxes. Very few sales would see an increase under Obama's proposal to raise the capital gains rate."

Yet another ad claims that Obama "promises more taxes on small businesses, seniors, your life savings, and your family." Fact Checker says that's untrue for the vast majority of small businesses, seniors and individual taxpayers, who would see their taxes go down under Obama's actual plan. He proposes (once again for the intentionally dense) to increase taxes only for those with more than $250,000 in family income, or $200,000 in individual income.

Alternatively, regarding energy policy – tire inflation gauges notwithstanding -- a McCain ad shows pictures of wind-driven turbines while the narrator says: "Renewable energy to transform our economy, create jobs and energy independence, that's John McCain." In fact, his energy plan doesn't specify any new federal spending for renewable energy and says only that he'd "rationalize" existing tax credits to provide incentives. In the past, however, he's opposed extending such tax credits when paid for by tax increases elsewhere.

This must be the new Bush/Cheney standard for "straight talk".

George Duncan
Peterborough, NH

04.13.08

Vote From the Bottom Up

Regina Vorce and Peter Leishman are running for NH State Representative. Regina is running for her first term and Peter is a 4-term incumbent. They are two of those names near the bottom of the ballot that would be easy to miss. Yet, they are two of those whose dedication to the families in this region is felt at the most basic levels of our quality of life; home and school.

Regina, for example, has an eye on the foreclosures that are happening – and will continue to happen – in our area. Foreclosures destroy families. From home to work to school, every aspect of life is negatively impacted. Regina would like to establish a review board that would determine whether the homeowner was the victim of a fraudulently structured or "scam" loan which might be rearranged so the family could stay in their home as new terms are negotiated.

It's an example of how Regina, a Democrat, approaches problems facing working families with solutions designed to help at the core level.

Likewise Peter Leishman fought to make public kindergarten mandatory statewide. The result was to bring kindergarten to the 12 towns in New Hampshire – including New Ipswich – that didn't have it. Despite general Republican opposition, he reached out to a Republican counterpart and under Governor Lynch's leadership, got it done.

Speaking of the Governor's leadership, Mark Fernald recently listed some of the measures brought to fruition by the Democratic majority in the State House. Says Mark, "They increased the minimum wage for the first time in over ten years. They defined and costed an adequate education, including the mandatory state-wide kindergarten mentioned above. Democrats passed green economy initiatives, establishing renewable portfolio standards and joining the Regional Greenhouse Gas Initiative with other Northeast states."

The Democratically controlled legislature also provided progressive, 21st century leadership by extending health insurance coverage on family plans to divorced spouses and young adults up to age 26, providing an R&D tax credit for businesses in NH, bringing Constitutional equality to same-sex partners, and protecting public health with a smoking ban in restaurants. Other initiatives include establishing funding for the Land and Community Heritage Investment Program.

If this is kind of heads-up activity you want in Concord, vote the November ballot from the bottom up so you don't overlook any of these outstanding Democratic candidates.

George Duncan
Peterborough, NH

11.06.08

Watch out for whiplash

Don't stand next to John McCain the next several weeks; you might get hit by the whiplash as he tries to put lipstick on his pig of an anti-regulatory history. Or "economic malpractice" as Frank Rich calls it.

The guy who for 26 years has been the cheerleader – together with his chief financial advisor, Phil Gramm – for the Laissez faire, free market, non-regulated policies that got us into this debacle, now wants us to believe that, if elected, he'll "shake them up" in Washington, whatever that means. Oh, he's shocked, shocked to discover there's greed going on in Wall Street, and he's going to put an end to it! What's next, repeal original sin? He just discovered that, as president, he couldn't even fire his knee-jerk scapegoat, SEC Chairman Chris Cox. Said the Wall Street Journal, "This assault on Mr. Cox is both false and deeply unfair. It's also un-Presidential."

Then, after doing a 180 on regulation sounding like Huey Long, he has the gall to try pinning the current disaster on Barack Obama! He also can't stop lying about Barack's tax plan, repeating his stupid $42K charge, despite numerous press and media statements to the contrary. He has Bush disease; the belief that if he says it, it must be true. And don't forget, this is the market this genius still wants to give our social security to.

The Huffington Post put it best: "Conservative Republicans always want the government to stay out of business and avoid regulation as long as they are making lots of money. When their greed, however, gets them into a fix, they are the first to cry out for rules and laws and taxpayer money to bail out their businesses. Obviously, Republicans are socialists. Taxpayers didn't get to enjoy any of the big money profits…but we get the privilege of paying for their debt and failures."

By the way, this year, there's no Democratic "straight ticket" box, so to help the people of NH, vote from the bottom up: Deborah Pignatelli for Executive Council, "Jill" Shaffer Hammond, Anne-Marie Irwin, Peter Leishman and Regina Vorce for state reps, Steve Spratt for state senate, Carol Shea-Porter and Paul Hodes for Congress, Jeanne Shaheen for Senate, John Lynch, Governor and Barack Obama for the change we so desperately need.

George Duncan
Peterborough, NH

07.08.08

Assigning Blame

In assigning blame for George Bush's illegal, anti-constitutional, immoral and incompetent administration, there is clearly enough of it to go around, particularly among arrogant neocons, the Stepford Republicans in Congress and even some Democrats. There is one individual, however, who shares more blame than most and that is George H.W. Bush, the father. Why?

Because he knew.

More than anyone else in this country – including "Dubya" himself (isn't that cute?) – Bush the elder knew, or should have known, the unmitigated disaster George Jr. was capable of visiting upon the presidency and the people of the United States. He knew about the drinking and the Texas cowboy mindset that went with it. (I spent almost a year in Austin, and even in that supposed "liberal" bastion, Texas' animosity toward the human race seeps into the atmosphere.)

Bush Sr. knew about the BCCI/Harken deals at Midland, the Texas Rangers hustle and much more. He knew about the Air National Guard incident and, as a pilot himself, was uniquely qualified to appreciate the gravity of a pilot being grounded. No pun. He also knew what happened to the records. The Air Force doesn't "lose" personnel jackets.

One word from George H.W. Bush at any point in George Jr.'s odyssey could have ended it. But he said nothing and allowed his son to embarrass himself, his father and his country. (Any responsible American who isn't embarrassed by this administration's global conduct hasn't been overseas yet.)

During the recent Martin Luther King anniversary I was reminded of Bull Conner who, in his ignorance, loosed his dogs upon the people only to end up facilitating the very racial progress he so desperately wanted to derail. I hope that George Bush's presidency has a similar effect; that his excesses of ignorance, arrogance and dishonesty, his and Cheney's lust for power and the rest results in a re-consideration of the role of the presidency in America and a re-balancing of the separation of powers that puts the people's representatives back into the policy mix, more answerable to the voters than to the party.

Then it will be our own fault if we elect to the Congress people who fail us.

George Duncan
Peterborough, NH

2.25.08

Down and Dirty

Now that the people see that John McCain has no answers for their concerns save flag-waving rhetoric and his poll numbers take a nose dive, McCain and his Rovian advisors are turning from a campaign for the presidency to become spoilers of the democratic process. Not that McCain had that far to go after the relentless barrage of attack ads and smarmy statements of recent weeks, but with nothing of consequence to offer, his final gasp is to go down and dirty. The kickoff is an article in the Times quoted by Hockey Mommy Palin who has apparently discovered the newspaper which she patronizingly says "can't be wrong." The piece lays out the facts about Obama's arm's length and occasional contacts over the years with Bill Ayers, a 60s radical and bomber who has since rehabilitated himself and gained prominence in Chicago. If, in fact, she read the piece, Palin failed to mention that the Times investigators found nothing of significance to report saying "the two men do not appear to have been close." They haven't even spoken in more than three years said the Times, yet Palin characterizes their relationship as "paling around," present tense. Using Palin's reasoning, it could be said that in Vietnam, McCain spent five years consorting with the enemy.

One can only hope that McCain's campaign of character assassination will say more to voters about him than it does about Obama. There comes a time, as Barack said earlier, when enough is enough. If you have nothing positive to offer, don't insult the intelligence of the voters with an endless stream of convoluted thinking and false, incoherent charges. C'mon, John, give us a break!

George Duncan
Peterborough, NH

10.04.08

Principles or Personalities?

It's hard to know what to make of the orchestration of cynicism, hypocrisy, convoluted reasoning, cheap shots and outright lies that comprised the Republican convention.

McCain campaign director Rick Davis said, "This election isn't about issues, it's about personalities." And judging from the made for TV movie the Republicans call a convention, he got it right. So if you care about the economy, affordable healthcare, an honorable end to the Iraq war, womens' right to choose, middle class tax relief, jobs and the rest of the issues this election will address, don't ask the Republicans. They're suddenly into "change" – of what they don't say, unless it's the Republican dominated administration and Congress of which McCain was a reliable participant. They're going to "stand up for America." Uh-Huh. They're going to "shake things up." Ooooo. The bulk of McCain's speech was a standard recitation of conservative boilerplate. You know, the Bush-Cheney policies that got us where we are.

Speaking of pigs, the distortions in McCain-Palin's current claims to maverickdom mindlessly chanting "change, change, change" remind me of George Orwell's pigs, Napoleon and Squealer, famously reciting "Four legs good, two legs bad" until it started to make sense.

Observers have lost count of the times Palin has repeated her lie about refusing that "bridge to nowhere" since being nominated, until it finally reached the mainstream press, but not Mr. McCain, apparently. (Congress scrapped the bridge, not she, but she still took the $300 million earmarked for it, said the WSJ.) She certainly does a good introduction for her "running mate" – whatsiz-name.

As Gary Kiyama wrote on Salon: "The tough-talking, gun-toting 'hockey mom' who believes that America's wars are God's will has restarted the culture wars so beloved of Republicans, and shifted the election from being about issues into a personality contest."

George Bush was thought to be a guy you'd like to have a beer with, remember? That worked well, didn't it? If we're really going to select our president and vice president on the basis of appearances and personality, God help us.

George Duncan
Peterborough, NH

9.09.08

Senator McSame

Ben Stein, son of Republican economist Herb Stein and one of the staunchest of that tribe, writes in a recent WSJ column that "The Republican Party (my party and yours) has for the last 30 years or so been operating under a demonstrably false and misleading premise: that tax cuts pay for themselves by generating so much economic growth that they replace the sums lost by tax cutting." He then shows that it took six years for the Bush tax cuts of 2000 to reach the revenue levels of the last year of the Clinton Administration, despite a 30 percent increase in GDP during the same period. "In other words," Stein continues, "Tax cuts do not pay for themselves, at least not on any basis that I can see." Yet here comes Senator McSame touting the Bush tax cuts as a source of increased revenue. Yikes!

The other slice of the baloney sandwich is the issue of free markets self-correcting. Maybe, if you count a crash (1929) and a recession (the high tech bubble in 2001 and mortgages today) as a self-correction. Says George Soros on Bloomberg TV: "Unfortunately, we have an idea of market fundamentalism, now the dominant ideology, holding that markets are self-correcting; and this is false because it's generally the intervention of the authorities that saves the markets when they get into trouble." Yet there goes McSame touting Bush's free market policies so the administration's corporate buddies won't be inconvenienced by anything as tacky as responsibility to the people. It should be painfully clear by now that free markets don't compete; driven by the need to maximize profits, they collude.

How about foreign policy? Surely the old war horse has some hard earned wisdom there. Yet with "bomb, bomb, bomb Iran" playing in the background, McSame proposes nothing less than expelling Russia and excluding China from the G8, the group of advanced industrial countries. Newsweek commentator Fareed Zakaria states that "what McCain suggests is a policy of active exclusion and hostility toward two major global powers. It is a policy that would alienate many countries in Europe and Asia who would see it as an attempt by Washington to begin a new cold war."

And now to top it off, he insults our intelligence with a gas tax hoax. By George, he's learning three-card monte even faster than Bush did!

George Duncan
Peterborough, NH

5.09.08

The One Trick Pony and Rev Huckabee

Listening to John McCain this past weekend, it appears to me that his heroic dedication to duty and the nation notwithstanding, as a candidate for president he's really a one trick pony – and it's a nasty trick indeed. War, war and more war is what the candidate promised. Iraq is not over, he makes clear, despite the fact that, according to him, "the surge is working, the surge is working, the surge is working." Oh, yeah? Where's the unity in the Iraqi government it supposed to produce? Sunnis and Shiites are still at each other's throats and the Kurds want nothing to do with either of them. McCain goes on to promise "more wars" in the years ahead. To pay for them he plans to make the Bush tax cuts permanent. An economist he ain't.

Then there's the reverend Huckabee. He only wants to enlist us all as "soldiers for Christ in God's Army" and "take this nation back to Christ." My Jewish friends are beginning to feel like illegal aliens.

Many religiously tinged policies are often lumped under the term "socially conservative." Makes them sound like a simple difference of opinion. Fact is, though, they aren't. They're contrary to the Constitution and we need to pay attention. Anything religious is difficult to oppose. It sounds like you're against God, which, of course, is convoluted thinking. Often intentionally so.

You would think that those who would bring religion into the public square might learn something from watching the Iraqi meltdown these past four years. One can only hope that public officials with a religious bent would use their faith to inform their compassion in dealing with the 40 million of Americans that live below the poverty line and 47 million with no health insurance. But as dedicated religionists like Jack Abramoff, George W. Bush and Tom Delay among others indicates, ethical behavior in office may be too much to hope for.

For those who dig numbers, we have documentation at last of the Bush/Cheney lie machine: 935 lies by painstaking count of the Center for Public Integrity leading to almost four thousand dead American soldiers. Now there's a legacy!

George Duncan
Peterborough, NH

1.27.08

What Barack Might Have Said

Q: Senator Obama, it's been noted that you decline to wear an American Flag pin in your lapel. Do you not honor the American Flag? If you do, why do you refuse to wear a pin?

A: It is precisely because I do honor the American Flag – and the nation and the democratic principles it represents – that I decline to wear the pin. Put simply, I choose to have my actions speak for my patriotism, rather than an object that anyone can purchase for a dollar which then ascribes to the user a wide range of beliefs, principles and values he or she may or may not share.

There is no better example than the fact that President George W. Bush and Vice President Dick Cheney, among others in the present administration, wear flag pins in their lapels. It demonstrates to me the ease with which that revered symbol can be exploited to create an illusion of patriotism and love of country by men who have worked assiduously to undermine and abuse it. These men wear the flag pin as an imprimatur – their American "brand," so to speak – in an effort to conceal the shoddy merchandise of this presidency and lend legitimacy to their cause. I would rather see our beloved standard waving proudly in the winds of freedom than have it become a cheap commercial appurtenance cynically bolstering the illegal, immoral, and unconstitutional acts of this arrogant cabal.

George Duncan
Peterborough, NH

4.22.08

A Matter of Judgment

It was most satisfying to see Barack Obama jerk the chain on the McCain attack dog at the VFW convention. It comes as Senator McCain is making an issue of his judgment, as he questions Obama's judgment. And what do these attack ads say about McCain's judgment in the first place? But let's take a look at some of this Maverick Warrior's other judgments.

At a hearing of the Senate Armed Services Committee, John McCain said, "The presence of additional coalition forces would allow the Iraqi government to do what it cannot accomplish today on its own: impose its rule throughout the country." Since we're still waiting for that to happen, how can McCain continue to judge the surge a success?

According to the New York Times, McCain was calling for an invasion of Iraq six months before Bush did. Six months before the attack, UN inspectors were still on the ground in Iraq searching for the non-existent WMD and on January 30, 2003, they declared that Iraq was "not in material breach" of their agreements. So what was the basis for McCain's "judgment"?

McCain offered total support for Rumsfeld's "small footprint" military strategy, despite heavy Pentagon opposition and the warnings of knowledgeable generals. Is that the judgment of a commander-in-chief?

Said the Times, "Five years after the invasion of Iraq," Mr. McCain stands by his support for the war and expresses no regrets about his advocacy." That's a double whammy in poor judgment. First his knee-jerk judgment about the war itself, then refusing to reconsider his support despite subsequent revelations.

Even now, in addition to Iraq and Iran, McCain continues to promote an aggressive militarism towards North Korea, Syria and Serbia which he calls "rogue state rollback." Who's next, I wonder, Tierra del Fuego?

When Russia used the South Ossetia uprising as an excuse to invade Georgia, McCain was out of the gate even before the administration, six guns at the ready like a latter day Yosemite Sam. That's judgement?

Now comes Sarah Palin, the token conservative base and PUMA bait. After one meeting and a phone call. That's judgement?

Joe Biden said in his acceptance speech that "These times require more than a good soldier. They require a wise leader." Amen. And what we don't need is yet another Cheney class cynic and belligerent militarist.

George Duncan
Peterborough, NH

8.24.08

Bush imprisons more than 2500 children.

According to veteran investigative journalist David Lindorff on Common Dreams, (commondreams.com), the US government's own figures show that more than 2500 kids 17 years and younger have been held since 2001 as "enemy combatants" — often for over a year, and sometimes for over five years. At least eight of those children, some as young as 10, were held at Guantanamo at a special camp for kids: Camp Iguana. One of those kids committed suicide at the age of 21, after spending five years in confinement at Guantanamo. Tragically, reports Lindorff, the boy had been found innocent only two weeks previously and was due for release, but nobody bothered to tell him.

That such an obscenity could exist under US sanction speaks to a number of things. First, of course, is the craven behavior of this administration. Second is the degree to which Bush's criminal activities are going unchallenged. Lindorff points out that since 1949, under the Geneva Conventions signed and adopted by the US, and incorporated into US law under the Constitution's supremacy clause, children under the age of 15 are classed as "protected persons," and even if captured while fighting against US forces are to be considered victims, not POWs. In 2002, says Lindorff, the Bush administration signed an updated version of that treaty, raising the "protected person" age to all those "under 18." Instead, he says, they were treated as the enemy, to be destroyed.

We've already seen that treaties don't mean much to this president and vice president, or to the rest of the administration, but they should mean something to the rest of us. And behavior of this sort should be exposed by the media, not hidden away in a blog.

Maybe the good folks at The Parent Center could try parenting at a distance in this matter and bring it to the attention of the media so it might find the cleansing effect of sunlight. Frankly, the grotesqueries of this administration have become so numerous, it seems to me, that they have numbed our sense of outrage and situations such as this have taken on all the shock effect of wallpaper. We need to speak up, even if the media won't.

George Duncan
Peterborough, NH

5.23.08

Because they said so?

In discussing the detentions of people in Guantanamo, government lawyers and others constantly refer to them as "enemy combatants." Isn't that part of what the government has to prove? Under habeas corpus, don't they have to go to court and show cause for holding someone? Now a federal appeals court has made the distinction in the case of Huzaifa Parhat, a Chinese Uighur. He was determined to be an enemy combatant by a tribunal that relied heavily on questionable evidence in classified documents, the appeals court found.

The ruling, the first successful appeal of a detainee's designation as an enemy combatant, ordered the government to release, transfer or hold a new hearing for Parhat.

The opinion, says a Washington Post story, could have broad implications for scores of other detainees classified as enemy combatants by Bush's Combatant Status Review Tribunals. "The opinion is also likely to guide federal judges weighing evidence in up-coming hearings," says the Post.

The judges were particularly concerned, the Post said, with government assertions that the evidence was reliable because it was repeated in separate documents and that officials would not have included the information if it were not dependable.

"Lewis Carroll notwithstanding," wrote Judge Merrick B. Garland, quoting from Carroll's poem 'The Hunting of the Snark,' the fact the government has 'said it thrice' does not make an allegation true."

Isn't it refreshing to know that even in the looking glass world of George Bush, not everyone is asleep at the switch, and this is still a nation of laws, not of his and Cheney's fascistic, convoluted thinking.

George Duncan
Peterborough, NH

04.2208

Birth Control and Abortion

It seems unbelievable, but the Bush Administration is quietly trying to redefine "abortion" to include birth control.

The Houston Chronicle says this could wipe out dozens of state laws that protect women's reproductive freedom and protect rape victims.[1] Access to basic health care for millions of women would be jeopardized. And it's being pushed as a "rule change"—meaning, it doesn't need congressional approval.

Here's what some others are saying about this proposal:

The draft regulation would define birth control as abortion...it could deny access to critical family planning for women across the country.—Letter signed by Barack Obama, Hillary Clinton, and 26 other senators.[2]

The draft rule could void laws in 27 states that require insurance companies to provide birth control coverage for women requesting it [and] laws in 14 states requiring that rape victims receive counseling and access to emergency, day-after contraceptives.—Houston Chronicle editorial[3]

The administration needs to stop playing word games with women's health and state clearly they will reject any regulations that will undermine women's access to basic health care.—Cecile Richards, president of Planned Parenthood Federation of America.[4]

[It's] a spectacular act of complicity with the religious right... —RH Reality Check, Information and Analysis for Reproductive Health[5]

The birth control pill, the IUD, and emergency contraception might all become unavailable—illegal—as a result.—Brigid Riley, executive director of a Minnesota teen pregnancy prevention organization[6]

George Duncan
Peterborough, NH

05.23.08

The Detour Express

John McCain's Straight Talk Express seems to be taking a rather bumpy detour these days. While junior psychologists on both sides of the aisle fuss and fume over his recent attack ads, the general consensus seems to be that they say more about McCain than they do about Obama.

Which wouldn't be difficult, since they say nothing of consequence about Obama other than to offer the rhetorical question, "Is he ready to lead?" The rhetorical answer, for those who recall Bush's credentials might be, "Why not?" Rhetorical questions like this are a familiar tactic, bringing to mind the TV news show that recently tried to capitalize on anxiety in viewers with a provocative weather announcement, "Clear and dry tomorrow – but will it last?"

Sadly though, race-based advertising like the McCain ads are likely to hurt Obama in the long run. The real tragedy is how media-whipped the electorate has become with spot TV ads raising and lowering poll results almost at will for people who refuse to separate the frivolous from important issue-based content.

More serious than the ads is McCain's reputation – so far unchallenged – as a supporter of veterans, a market, the Palm Beach Post points out, that McCain's militaristic stance should have cornered. Apparently, however, a lot of veterans disagree. Checking the Web site for The Iraq and Afghanistan Veterans of America, I was stunned to discover that Senator Warrior rates no more than a "D" For his anti-veteran voting record. What's more, Barack Obama rates a "B plus." In fact, several liberal congressmen rank well above their flag-waving conservative colleagues in the eyes of the veterans group. The Disabled American Veterans give McCain 20% and Obama 80%!

Who knew?

But the biggest lie is probably McCain's push for offshore drilling as a solution to $4.00 a gallon gas, supported by the bobble head Republicans' Kabuki dance in Congress. What a fraud! According to the U.S. Department of Energy's Energy Information Administration (EIA), the total amount of oil that this drilling would produce at peak 20 years from now would be less than 0.2 percent of world production. This would be too small to have any significant effect on the price of oil or gasoline, according to the EIA. What's more, oil is sold on a worldwide spot market. The U.S has no control over the price. But these are Bush-Cheney Republicans. Why start telling the truth now?

George Duncan
Peterborough, NH

07.02.08

Stop the Smear Merchants

A cartoon in the June 23 Newsweek shows what appears to be that stupid woman on Fox who tried to turn the Obamas' friendly "fist bump" into a secret terrorist signal (yes, she did). In a followup frame it has her saying "And there are rumors (Barack) has fathered two black children."

The incident itself is an example of just how low these conservative trogodolites will stoop in an attempt to smear Barack Obama – and his wife in the bargain. Over the next five months we can expect the knuckle-dragging neanderthals of the Republican Party to crawl out from under their rocks to make up any lies they think they can sell and email them around the Internet. The morons pre-disposed to believe this stuff keep the ball rolling until some mainstream media patsy feels obliged to ask the candidate or one of his key surrogates about it and the lie becomes "news."

And often enough, sadly, it does sell. Like original sin, we all carry some small tinge of racism within us, like it or not. It would be hard not to given the history of race in this country. As Rosalind Carter once said of Ronald Reagan, "he makes us comfortable in our prejudices."

The best response to this calumny is to ignore it. Starve it of currency. Refuse to forward such emails, even as a gag. The next best, I thought, was suggested by Rachel Maddow (Air America and MSNBC). Expose the creators of these rumors wherever possible. When your intelligence is insulted by the conservative bobble heads on trash radio and TV, email the station and let them know you're not amused. Insist they provide proof. It's more work, but it would also be effective to write or email the advertisers on these TV and radio stations that seem to dwell on this swill.

Do we really want our governance determined by lies, false analogy and innuendo, however slick? Do we want our presidential campaigns based on ad hominum attacks and meaningless ephemera? The only way they'll stop is when it doesn't work. The only way it won't work is if we reject it, loudly and clearly -- and hold the liars responsible where it counts – at the ballot box.

George Duncan
Peterborough, NH

6.15.08

What lessons have we learned?

The human race crawled out of the primordial ooze roughly 50 million years ago, and John McCain is returning us to it in the course of a single campaign. There's not much more to say about the bankruptcy of the McCain campaign. From his cynical, even insulting choice of running mate to his dishonorable, slanderous attacks on Obama, he has been rejected by platoons of Republican and conservative politicians, commentators, editorial boards and more in every corner of America. As many as 25 newspapers that formerly supported George Bush have come out against McCain and for Obama, as did General Colin Powell. So it's hardly the work of a liberal cabal.

Measures of the man include his and his running mate's encouragement of negativity toward Obama in particular and liberals in general. We're seeing how it leads to extremist views like the North Carolina congressman who opined that "liberals hate real Americans," a Florida congressman who accuses Obama of being a Communist and the Minnesota congresswoman who wants an investigation of the Congress to determine – in the best McCarthyist traditions – who among them are "anti-America." Palin herself likes to note how happy she is to be in the "real America" which seems to be any town where they boo in response to her attacks and cheer mindlessly at the appropriate cliches. (When Obama hears boos from his audience, he stops them saying, "no, we don't need that, we just need you to vote.")

According to current polls, the people are turning away from McCain – and especially Palin – in a meaningful way, so perhaps the Maverick will have sown the seeds of his own destruction.

But what are the larger lessons learned for the rest of us? For me, it starts with the proven poverty of conservative governance in addressing human needs, together with conservative animus toward anything that smacks of liberalism. They immediately label it socialism or even communism. (Medicare anyone? Social Security? Progressive income tax? Minimum wage? Unemployment benefits?)

Let's pay attention to what actually works best for most – independent of the rhetoric and the labels. "There is a principle," Herbert Spenser wrote, "which is a bar against all information, which is proof against all arguments and which cannot fail to keep a man in everlasting ignorance – that principle is contempt prior to investigation."

George Duncan
Peterborough, NH

10.21.08

Last letter

As the campaign ended, I felt for a while like a lighthouse keeper whose revolving beam with its head-shattering whap!...whap!...whap! had suddenly gone silent. Obama's speeches were no less strident than McCain/Palin, of course, but the Republicans' speeches were so larded over with misinformation, distortions of Obama's positions, "smear grenades" as Jon Stewart called them, and cheap bravado, it was like taking a swill shower every time they stepped before a microphone. I believe the negativity contributed significantly to McCain's loss.

But there are a few less tangible results that may prove just as beneficial to the country going forward. For one, we are free of the threat of a Sarah Palin presidency, at least for the foreseeable future, and perhaps of a Joe the Plumber Secretary of Commerce.

Whew! Also the Republican slander campaign is silenced. What a disgusting, dishonorable display of pure evil that was. From Liddy Dole's scurrilous robo-calls slandering Kay Hagan to the daily platoons of McCain surrogates polluting the airwaves with their denials, doubletalk and black-is-white lies, I kept waiting for the Mad Hatter and White Rabbit to show up. And it's worth noting that this kind of attack campaign is almost exclusively Republican.

Also virtually exclusive to the Republicans are the most heinous tactic of all, the deceptive robo-call targeting mostly students and minorities and lying to them about times and places and eligibility rules in an attempt to discourage or deny them their votes. Most heinous because these calls attack not just the voters or the candidates, but the democratic system itself which we all rely upon as the bed rock of our democratic society and, I might add, for which millions have given their lives. And these Republican creeps dare to accuse Democrats of "hating America."

Are there no honorable Republicans who will stand up to these creeps and tell them to stop it? Is there no one in the Republican party who will identify these hate mongers and take steps to shut them down in future elections? That the tactics did not work, doesn't seem to be a deterrent. Maybe the disapproval of peers and colleagues would have some effect.

George Duncan
Peterborough, NH

08.24.08

Afterword

Liberals are dedicated to enriching the whole society by helping the middle class, which is the engine of wealth in America, and the disadvantaged. The middle class is to the American economy what the rainforest is to the environment. But since Democrats can't do it alone, that puts them in the position of trying to persuade others to share a portion of what they have through taxes in order to help their fellows. To agree with that idea requires, I believe, a certain level of enlightenment. To understand that, as a chain is only as strong as its weakest link, so a society is only as strong as its weakest members. And by helping to elevate the less advantaged, we elevate us all. Conservatives are dedicated to so-called "trickle down" economics in which by increasing the wealth of the wealthiest among us, it will somehow trickle down to the middle class. They call this "fiscal responsibility" or what I see as "every man for himself." There is no known example of the "trickle down" idea actually bearing fruit. Nevertheless, conservatives have the advantage. It's easier to exhort people to "keep what's theirs" and that they know what's best for themselves – despite daily evidence that many, in fact, do not. Nevertheless it works to the degree that it appeals to that streak of selfishness found in all of us.

On George Stephanopolis's Sunday show, Conservative George Will recently opined that the natural state of the world is conflict while the liberal Adrianna Huffington countered that the natural state of the world is to seek harmony. This, in my view, is the classic distinction between conservatives and liberals. Conservatives believe the world is a dangerous place – constantly in conflict – and while there is clearly danger in the world, liberals believe in the fundamental goodness, inherent wisdom and positive purpose of the universe.

Those who live in fear, however expressed, must therefore protect what they have – with guns if necessary. Hence the obvious militarism that marks conservative thought and deed and by simple extension, Dick Cheney's "dark side" of governance.

The polls two days before the inauguration showed Obama taking office with 72% declaring their support for government programs to alleviate current and future crises, putting the lie to those conservatives who are trying to paint the nation as right of center. Saint Reagan had it right when he said that government was the problem as he blithely tripled the national debt. For the last eight years conservative government certainly has been the problem, and now the nation is looking to the power of democratic government to provide solutions.

By the time you read this we will be well into Barack Obama's first term and while it's doubtful that much will have been resolved – given the incredible problems Bush and his conservative acolytes left for him – you will probably be in a position to determine for yourself how you prefer to live.

Thank you for reading my letters.

George Duncan